THOUGHT LEADERSHIP

Disrupting the Status Quo in Organizations to Ignite Change

Rose I. Wilkins, Ph.D.

EDUCATION PUBLISHING SERVICES

Thought Leadership
Disrupting the Status Quo in Organizations to Ignite Change
by Rose I. Wilkins, Ph.D.

Published by:
ItsMyCareer Education Publishing Services
Atlanta, Georgia 30339
www.ItsMyCareerActivityBooks.com

ISBN 978-0-692-12612-7

FIRST EDITION: May 2018
10 9 8 7 6 5 4 3 2 1

Thought Leadership books are available at quantity discounts when utilized to promote products or services.

Dedication

This book is dedicated to my son Ernest, an aspiring leader who recognizes that creativity counts and disrupting the status quo comes with an opportunity for learning, a "why not" mindset and commitment to change.

Preface

A primary reason for this book is grounded in our belief that creating change in an organization is one of the most difficult challenges that leaders confront. This challenge cuts across domains, sectors, or organized groups, regardless of purpose. It is reasonable to assume that avoiding change in our increasingly complex world is virtually impossible since change is a common thread that runs through our lives regardless of background, age, status or circumstances. Our lives are filled with an onslaught of influence, requiring adaptation to rapid-pace changes in most of what we do. Living in a technology-driven, globally-connected society impacts the way we live and work. Ever-changing technological advancements have created landscape changes in nearly every industry, requiring different approaches, skill sets, and a different style of leadership. Yet, despite significant changes, some things remain the same. This is especially true in business where people still require managing, change is difficult, stakeholders want their needs met, consumers want the best services and products that don't fail, competition is constant, and the bottom line still matters.

Even in a technology-driven society, these realities require navigating the maze of business with a human-centered perspective. One challenge for leaders in organizations is that being human-centered comes with the reality of ensuring that internal and external people are satisfied. This is an arduous task because people come with thoughts, attitudes, feelings and are motivated by a barrage of influences, which may shift their level of motivation and commitment to change at an any time. Consequently, the greatest asset or liability of an organization is its human capacity, leaving leaders to confront many conundrums when moving ideas along or enacting sustainable change. One strategy that is being widely adopted in response to challenges in organizations is to reduce bureaucracy by cutting layers of management and embracing participative leadership that includes diverse members of the organization.

Leaders adopting this new approach are creating change with disruptive thinking about how things are done. Innovative leaders who construct disruptive thinking not only conceive provoking ideas, but also amass substantial followers that support their products or services and subsequently shift mindsets to embrace change. This fascinating group, who are recognized as the experts or go-to individuals accomplish this exclusionary status through thought leadership. This book examines the phenomenon of thought leadership, offering a practical perspective about how thought leaders provoke disruptive thinking, move ideas along and succeed at creating a new paradigm that embraces change. It is our intent to examine thought leadership as a viable approach that any organization can use in its effort to effect change.

This book is written for entrepreneurs, organizational leaders, public officials or any individual seeking to launch a new idea or engage organizational members in change initiatives, problem-solving, formulating a business or leadership strategy or shifting the paradigm to achieve operational or performance goals.

In effort to provide a doable thesis, we draw from literary works of contributors who have engaged in empirical investigation of traditional leadership principles and thought leadership as well as individuals who are ranked among the world's premiere experts in leadership development, motivation, influencing followers, innovation and change facilitation. We also provide some strategies that thought leaders and change agents employ when leading teams to move ideas from conception to sustainability.

We hope that this book inspires leaders to embrace disruptive thinking, collective thought, diversity and collaboration as viable tools to enhance motivation, engagement, productivity and change as needed. We also hope that our work will motivate creativity, ignite a spark for change, and activate action plans for individuals with Big Ideas. We believe that thought leadership offers a springboard that allows anyone to create change and a get-it-done mindset around an idea and codify systems that will sustain it. Best thoughts as you begin or travel on a pathway of creative and provocative thought.

Rose Irby-Wilkins
The Irby Wilkins Group, Inc.

Roots of the Book

Thoughts in this book reflect both a passion for leading change and my long-term experience watching actions of others, and too often pondering the question: "What led to that thinking and action?" Given the fact that most of my professional career was spent in schools, this question was often posed in response to evidence that a thought had gone to a level of an undesirable attachable action, which in many cases required adjustments. Although my exciting days of being a school leader required continuous creative thought, I have been profoundly inquisitive about thoughts that have a far-reaching impact. Like others, I often see or experience something and wonder about the innovative idea that brought it forth, while also pondering why I didn't come up with the idea. It was my inquisitiveness that led to serendipity of the terms, "thought leader" and thought leadership". Investigation of the concept led to an interesting point of differentiating between the terms, "thought leader" and "innovator "or "influencer".

While, the body of information indicates that a thought leader can be either, being an innovator or expert does not necessarily mean that the creative individual is considered a thought leader. This discovery led to my decision to pursue the "exclusive categorization" further and inspired interest in sharing ideas about this fascinating phenomenon from my point of view.

Plan For The Book

First, it is important to begin with a disclosure, making it clear that my knowledge on the topic thought leadership is fluid. Yet, investigating the concept led to a consideration that thought leadership could serve as a growth strategy or change strategy for organizations seeking to enhance performance, improve productivity, or improve culture. So, this book highlights several general proposals centered around the application of thought leadership as an internal strategy for organizations. To illustrate our point of view, I initially provide a brief discussion highlighting the magnitude of thoughts as drivers in our daily activities. Second, we discuss how our thoughts are influenced. Third, there is a discussion around some ideas to consider in shifting the way we think as well as how we manage and share our thoughts with others in a new age of rapid speed communication. We also examine descriptive and exclusionary traits of thought leaders that separate them from subject-matter experts, innovators or influencers. Some time is spent on a discussion of team building processes, since team selection, team capacity-building and consensus building are critically important in participative leadership. Finally, our proposal offers a framework for integrating the concept of thought leadership and collective thoughts into the broader fabric of organizational growth strategy and culture enhancement, by providing some useful strategies.

Whether individual or group, it is important to clarify that there is no intent to de-value the term "thought leader" or attempt to identify a procedural outline for development in thought leadership. In other words, this is not a ten-step process, descriptive course lecture series on how-to-become a thought leader, or an implication that a standardized development process exists in this realm of this distinctive group of leaders. However, it is possible to harness thoughts from diverse thinkers to impact change. This investigation of the topic seeks to build on this concept by aligning traits of thought leaders, with inclusion of diverse thinkers that engage others, influence change, and collective buy-in to ideas.

Our proposal explores the use of thought leadership as a tool to drive internal change or as a growth strategy in organizations based on how thought leaders incorporate thinking, influence followers, and work outside the proverbial box. We propose that the development of internal thought leadership cohorts as a strategy can serve to "activate" interest in change or "facilitate" development of creative ideas to assist change. Although there is clear evidence that thought leadership can emerge from a single individual who puts forth and codifies a breakthrough idea, organizations can also disrupt how things are done, by leveraging the ideas of collective individuals to create shifts in productivity and outcomes. This is important since a thought leader can detach from an organization at any time, leaving a void if a culture of collective thought has not been created. If a person leaves and capacity building has not taken place, changes may not be sustainable. In addition, if leadership is approached from this perspective, it is possible to develop ideas around processes that can be used to disrupt the status quo in individual functional processes, daily interactions, or flow of activities within groups. Shifting the paradigm by harnessing collective thought is critical in organizational enhancement and especially critical in current work environments, where there may be a mixture of cross-generational thinkers.

We also support the notion that new competitive marketplaces require destroying assumptions and beliefs that creating change in organizations is limited to ideas from those in assigned positions based on a hierarchical approach to leadership. While top-down directives have been the traditional approach to launching new ideas, using diverse members as creative assets or change agents can not only move ideas along, but also broaden the scope of what constitutes participative leadership within organizations.

This approach enhances the possibility of creativity that can reshape success for the entire organization. According to the 2016 Adobe State of Create Report, investing in creativity pays off. Businesses that invest in creativity increase employee productivity by 78% globally (88% US) and have happier employees, reporting that 76% of happier employees, globally and 85% happier in the US. The report also indicated that investing in creativity boosts potential success indicators in innovation, customer service and customer satisfaction, competitive edge and the bottom line-financial gains.

Another proposition focuses on building "learning organizations" where members continually expand their capacity to cultivate ideas that matter and create the results they truly desire. Case scenarios are used to illustrate certain aspects of contributing theories, best practices and strategies that support elements of thought leadership. By following this framework, we answer questions centered on inclusion of diverse thinkers and how to build stronger internal success networks through collective thinking about organizational issues, goals and intrinsic ideas. The essential theme which serves as a probing point throughout the book is selective change in the way everyday issues are approached and resolved. An essential question to keep in mind is "How can organizational leaders use internal cohorts to shape thoughts into collective ideas that influence positive individual change or changes in organizational performance outcomes, growth, and overall improvement?"

Exploring answers to this question is revealed through discussions of thought leadership as a tool for personal and organizational growth. Several viewpoints will emerge by exploring thought leadership from this perspective:

- *Traditional leadership approaches tend to promote environments that force people to work harder. This can lead to mediocrity because these systems often fail to tap into the spirit of collective intelligence, creativity, and collaborative efforts.*

- *Whether operating in the role of leader or follower, fertile listening and critical thinking enhance the potential for positive outcomes.*

- *When organizational members share ideas and begin to work together, there is more buy-in, satisfaction with outcomes, and feelings of belonging, which enhance overall productivity. This is how to sustain change.*

- *Leadership does not operate as an isolated trait of individuals assigned to certain roles/positions but should operate with synergy as a systematic approach working things in an effective manner.*

- *If organizations operate as learning organizations, there is no ultimate destination or end state since members continuously grow and seek new opportunities for learning and change.*

- *Change is sustainable when time is allocated to collect and nourish new ideas, and massage the impact of change internally, before expanding the message of ideas for external review.*
- *Allocating time to enable creativity of members can enhance productivity, employee satisfaction, and financial profits.*

Finally, ideas to promote thought leadership as a strategy can be used by any type of organization, so our proposal provides some strategies to support that effort.

Introduction

Everything begins with a simple thought.

What are you thinking right now? Can you remember what your thoughts were a few minutes ago or how many thoughts you have had in the last hour, day or week? The answer is "NO", and you probably won't remember each thought from the last 15 minutes and certainly not in the last hour. That's because our thoughts are continuous throughout the day and it is almost impossible to measure the exact number. According to recent neuroscience research, there is an ongoing debate about the number of thoughts an individual has per day. In 2005, the National Science Foundation released statistics, indicating that individuals think 1,000 thoughts per hour, but when individuals write they produce about 2,500 thoughts per hour and a half, which yields about 12,000 thoughts per day. A deeper thinker according to this report puts forth 50,000 thoughts per day. The estimated number of thoughts per day based on reports from Psychology Today is 70,000 per day. This data is supported by the Laboratory of Neuroimaging (LONI) at UCLA, where faculty completed some preliminary studies using undergraduate student volunteers. These results are not peer-reviewed/published.

While the number varies, quantifying the number of thoughts that an individual has per day is much like the old riddle, which questions whether a tree makes a sound in a forest when it falls, if no one is there to hear it. Like, the riddle, it is difficult to measure thoughts since individuals have the option of sharing thoughts or keeping quiet about them. In other words, how do we know what people are thinking if they choose not to share?

However, regardless of how many thoughts we have, thoughts and ideas are the drivers of everything we do each day. Whether, it's the essential things that meet our basic needs, taking care of responsibilities or choosing those things that bring enjoyment for our desires, each was produced by a single thought that did not remain contained. This world of countless ordinary and extraordinary things began as simple ideas that were conceived, shared, developed, presented and accepted. When we reflect on the magnitude of things created and ongoing new emerging ideas, two essential questions likely informed each thought behind their origin: "What if"? or "Why not"? Both questions initiate the pathway for discovery and changes in the way things are viewed, done or accepted. So, these questions are where we begin discussions about the concept of "thought leadership".

What If? Why Not? Who's In? The Power of Asking Provoking Questions

We know that simple thoughts move to bigger ideas and act as catalysts that are continually reshaping the world and views. But not all simple thoughts will be a catalyst of change due to the continuous and massive flow of thoughts our minds produce. Thoughts in our minds are like a cat chasing one hundred mice around a room. Success in this case means focusing on one at a time, since it is virtually impossible to capture and digest one hundred. Likewise, without an awareness of how to cultivate a thought, how to adequately shape it to capture the attention of others and take actions that turn a simple thought into a bigger idea into reality, the thought will simply fade away. One way to shift thoughts to another level is by asking questions that bring them into focus. Whether it is an idea for individual change or one that touches lives across the globe, the questions, "What if?" and "Why not?" are provoking question-starters with the capacity to move an idea from a single thought to a pivotal change agent in our lives or the lives of others.

Moving thoughts along by asking questions involves more than simply putting a question mark at the end of a thought. Asking "what if "questions often create discomfort, since answers are not obvious and come with uncertainty about the future. Too often a thought emerges into an idea, but it is met with internal conflict about whether it's reasonable and possible; or there is external push back, lack of support, criticism and even responses from others that are callous and harsh. Yet, formulating the right questions can also lead to reflection on the past and challenge current assumptions to clarify or confirm what actions are required to move an idea along the path to realistic awareness for others. One way to move ideas along is by pondering questions such as "What if.. we did this or that.., approached it this way or tried something different?" or "Why not.. change how we do things, try a different approach or see what others think about this idea?" But it is important to remember that our brain is wired to generate thoughts at a rapid pace, so it is critical to allow adequate time to focus on creating viable answers by taking a deep-dive into creative thinking that can produce plausible outcomes. Keep in mind that, "what if" or "why not" questions act as cursors for sparking thoughts, but it will still be necessary to involve methodical thought processes when moving an idea from a simple thought to refinement.

Steve Quatrano, member of the Right Question Institute, a nonprofit research group, explains that the act of formulating questions enables us "to organize our thinking around what we don't know." Beginning at a place of the unknown is a great place to start since it offers an opportunity to dig deeper and that's what thought leaders do. They don't stop with a simple thought but thrust forward in search of answers, making the world a better place, not only because of the questions they ask but by the answers they produce. One way to visualize a thought leader is to think of a thought leader as a thought constructor, who builds an idea from conception to a distinctive level of understanding and acceptance. Given this fact, we can assume that the dimension of what constitutes a thought leader is continuously emerging each time a new idea springs forth and becomes the next wave of excitement, which could come at any time.

The list of people at this level requires no pedigree status, is open to everyone and it grows every day, but if you are thinking of adding your name to the list, know that exceptionality is a distinguishing trait. Also, the term "thought leader" is not a self-endowed classification, it's up to others to use the distinction. When utilizing the term based on organizational structures, almost every sector has a coterie of well-respected thought leaders and adding your name to this unique list is no easy feat. Yet, since everything begins with a simple thought, the door is always open for the next thought leader..but entering this unique realm requires much more than a mere thought.

Table of Contents

Part I
SOME THOUGHTS ABOUT OUR THOUGHTS

Chapter 1

Developing and Shaping Thought Processes

"Everything is figure-out-able" - Unknown

One afternoon during my tenure as a principal of an alternative school, I returned to campus from a meeting and found a female student rolling around on the floor screaming, as staff members made attempts to calm her down. When she saw me, she screamed, "Where you been, they made me mad! I am confused! I can't think straight! You know what to do..put me back together." My immediate thought was, what the hell, I really wish I could. But since she obviously believed I could, my response was, "Okay come on Sweetie, let's go into my office and put you back together." She immediately stopped screaming and followed me to my office.

After spending some time talking about the issue that caused her meltdown, she returned to a calm state and later returned to class. Reflecting on that time, often leaves me wishing it was that simple, when my thoughts are confusing, and I am trying to put myself back together. Fortunately, my brain is wired in a manner that allows me to undergo the necessary processes to maintain self-control, so that I don't flop out and roll around on the ground screaming - although the idea sounds intriguing in some cases. My ability to control my emotions is based on what cognitive scientists refer to as executive functioning and self-regulation skills.

There are different views about executive functioning, but most definitions note that executive functioning and self-regulation skills operate in sync and depend on three types of brain function: mental flexibility, working memory and self-control.

3

The three functions serve as a roadmap for guiding the flow of thoughts that we generate daily. They are extremely interrelated and must operate in coordination with each other to regulate our thoughts, decision-making and actions. Executive functioning is responsible for five skills that we utilize daily to control what we do and how we do it.

- *Paying attention*
- *Organizing and planning*
- *Initiating tasks and staying focused on them*
- *Regulating emotions*
- *Self-monitoring (keeping track of what you are doing)*

Research indicates opposing views about the origin of thoughts. Early cognitive scientists defined thoughts as activity that resides in the brain, but dozens of recent studies have challenged that view, suggesting instead, that human thoughts are intimately linked to our physical experiences. There is no intention here to support or argue either theory about the origin of thoughts, but scientists agree that the skills of brain functioning become evident early in life and enable children to manage their thoughts and emotions to get things done. According to the Harvard University Center on the Developing Child, executive functioning and self-regulating skills are the mental processes that enable individuals to plan, focus attention, remember instructions and juggle multiple tasks successfully. However, children are not born with these skills, they are born with the potential to develop them, and do so based on observing and interacting with others, especially parents and other influential people in their environment. Consider this example:

Scenario 1

Not long ago, while eating dinner at a restaurant, I observed what I assumed to be a family of four adults and one small child, who came in and were seated near me. Based on age indicators, I assumed the group to be grandparents, parents, and a baby about 10-months. The adults followed the basic routine of looking at menus and chatting, while the child sat quietly in a high chair. After ordering food and several minutes of uninterrupted chatter by the adults, the child picked up a napkin from the table and dropped it to the floor. Without hesitation, one of the assumed parents picked the napkin up and placed it back on the table. The child picked it up again and dropped it. A second adult quickly picked it up without hesitation and put it aside. The child then took a spoon and dropped it, one of the parents reached down, picked up the spoon, set it aside and handed the child a ring of keys, which she immediately looked at dropped to the floor. By now she had the attention of the assumed mother, who moved all table items from the child's reach and continued listening to the chatter. The child started crying loudly, gaining attention from the whole group of adults, and the assumed father took her from the high chair and rubbed her back to calm her down. She soon stopped crying and began playing with the father's hair, which led to him kissing her hand, rubbing her back and smiling at her.

Watching this scenario provided an opportunity to observe what I consider as an early stage of development in executive functioning. Children observe what others are doing, test limits, and soon become aware of how to obtain responses from those in their environment. When appropriate executive functioning is in place, children process information to solve problems and learn

5

quickly how to stimulate responses from adults. It also allows time for reflection - offering a chance for children to pause, think about their options, and put things in order before proceeding. In the scenario, although very young, the child decided to get attention and went about the process of getting it. As individuals grow and engage in more activities, the functions continue development, enabling greater possibilities for sorting out thoughts and making decisions based on observations, interactions, emotions, memory, processing and reflection. Consequently, being influenced by others or the level of that influence requires that executive functioning is operating effectively.

Why relate executive functioning to a discussion of thought leadership? The answer lies in the fact that executive functioning and self-regulating are at the core framework in the ability to influence or to be influenced. It enhances several areas related to functioning in day-to-day activities including the ability to modulate emotions, begin a task or independently, generate ideas, responses, and problem-solving strategies. Whether operating in a state of being a leader or follower, the skills of executive functioning and self-regulating are relevant to the process. Individuals pay attention to things in their surrounding and quickly formulate and organize thoughts, before planning how to respond. If emotions are attached to thoughts, the brain determines how those emotions will surface and the level of self-control that an individual will display in the situation. As an example, if information is shared that the brain processes and organizes as great news, an individual quickly expresses emotions of joy or sadness, anger or frustration if presented information is interpreted as bad news.

Revisiting the actions of my former student allows an opportunity to see how an individual with deficiencies in executive functioning will also demonstrate deficiencies in self-regulating skills. Everyday scenarios require the use of brain-based skills to process and act on stimuli that influence thoughts from many sources. Executive functioning provides the ability to stop inappropriate behaviors, including stopping actions based on thoughts. When executive functioning operates in a so-called state of normalcy, development of the five necessary skills begin early and continue development so that it is easy to routinely adjust and react to daily stimuli and develop appropriate patterns of thinking for the environment. This is true even when stimuli in the environment is frustrating, such as driving at a desirable speed, and suddenly there is a traffic jam. Even when frustrated, a driver with adequate development of the five skills of executive functioning and self-regulating skills will remain in the car, focus on something else such as the using their cell phone, and endure the lack of movement until the jam clears and traffic begins to move at a more desirable pace.

A Quick Reference List of Executive Functioning Abilities:

The following is a list of some abilities that operate under the umbrella of executive functioning.

• Planning and organization	• Flexible thinking
• Multi-tasking	• Self-awareness
• Learning rules	• Making decisions
• Solving problems	• Motivation

• Social behavior	• Controlling emotions
• Monitoring progress and performance	
• Initiating appropriate behavior	
• Inhibiting inappropriate behavior	
• Concentrating and taking in information	

In summary, executive functioning provides the internal mechanism that enables individuals to plan, focus attention, remember instructions and juggle multiple tasks successfully. It's like the conductor of an orchestra, who is responsible for directing the actions of musicians, so that instruments produce a unified sound rather than a loud clanging disconnected noise. These skills provide the framework for completing tasks, modulating emotions, and hold information in the mind to complete tasks. Individuals who lack executive functioning and self-regulating skills will experience difficulties in maintaining essentials skills of thought leadership. It becomes difficult on both sides of the thought leadership spectrum to manage ideas to a level of development required to shift the mindset of others as well as difficulties in managing thoughts that influence development of a new mindset. When considering the implication of executive functioning and self-control as related to thought leadership, can you imagine how an idea might flow when executive functioning is dysfunctional? Furthermore, can you imagine how difficult it would be to accomplish goals when cohort members cannot function due to issues related to executive functioning? Consider this carefully when selecting cohort members.

Chapter 2

Shaping Thought Patterns in a World of Influence

"Thought is a prerequisite for thought leadership"

Before reading further, take a moment to reflect on your activities today. Which activities did you complete that came from your fresh ideas? What activities did you complete based on the influence of others or things in your environment that developed from the thoughts of others? Regardless of items on your list, in either case, most of what we do is the result of influence. This is even more prevalent today in a rapidly-exchanging world where new technologies reimagine how we communicate, the way we think and interact, changing our behaviors in both obvious and subtle ways.

Everyday waves of information come from direct and indirect approaches to inform thought patterns. Despite the barrage of daily thoughts for everyone, very few occur as isolated ones in a world of fingertip access to information and social media dependent individuals. Some thoughts are influenced by subject-matter experts, who have influence due to significant trust based on their knowledge in a specific area. As an example, physicians influence thoughts about actions to enhance health and wellness, while meteorologists influence thoughts about what to wear in accordance with a weather forecast, even though we know their predictions are not always correct.

A surge of influence stems from creativity, where individual ideas or a continuous flow of innovative ideas influence what we do or how it is done. There is continuous innovation in cars, cell

9

phones that influence thoughts about the best option based on new features. In fact, disruption innovations such as fax machine, the internet and cell phones have destroyed old ways of doing things to updated versions. Innovators bring forth influential ideas in companies such as Google, as informational pools for quick gathering of details about any conceivable topic. In fact, Google embraces creativity at a level that allows time for organizational members to work on their own ideas.

As we move about our day, the greatest magnitude on thoughts come from direct influences of outside sources in the form or deliberate advertising, while subtle massaging of thought processes create unconscious patterns of behavior. It is easy to recognize direct approaches because companies spend millions in advertising or marketing each year to influence thinking about what we need, think we need, and when we need it. Familiar examples of direct approaches such as continuous updates of cell phones influence thoughts about the latest features being better than the last. Shoe companies influence thinking about how many pairs of athletic shoes the average youth should have, and the type based on awareness that shoe brands provide value in securing popularity among peers.

One familiar example of external indirect influences occurs at large chain-supply grocery stores. When a customer walks into a large grocery store, there is a tendency to turn right and move around the store from right to left. There are no signs that direct the pathway, but the store layout is intentional, so customers consistently comply unless an individual who is very familiar with the store layout and shelving aisles is shopping for one or two products. Marketing gurus are aware of quick shopping possibilities, so shelving space and aisles are periodically changed to influence additional time looking for that one item. If they are successful in influencing thinking, most customers will leave the store with more items than originally intended, so thoughts about shopping were indirectly influenced, by intentional influence.

These few examples are only a miniscule representation of the many ways everyday thoughts are influenced. Yet, although the level and frequency of direct and indirect approaches influence thought patterns, most influences of this type fail to meet the standard criteria for thought leadership. The primary difference is due to the intensity and focus of intentional influence. Generally, classification of a thought leader embodies individuals who generates original, brilliant ideas, whereas subject experts or influencers use their influence to promote discussions or engagement that support their ideas.

Thought leadership uses disruptive innovation to expand ideas that stray away from the norm, creating a new mindset that disrupts the status quo. Such is the case of Jeff Bezos, founder of Amazon, a thought leader visionary, who led Amazon to become the world's largest online shopping retailer. The leadership from Bezos took advantage of the expanded innovative technology wave and reimagined shopping, creating fingertip access to retail shopping, thus eliminating the need to travel to traditional retail stores. But when thought leadership is employed, visionary actions cover a broader scope than the production or launch of an idea.

Consideration is also given to developing systems that will enhance sustainability. Such is the case for thought leadership at Amazon, where visionary thought processes also shift how packages are delivered. To combat theft of purchased items, customers are offered a key-pad which allows items to be placed inside the home, have items placed in their vehicle upon delivery or customers may pick up items at Whole Foods, an Amazon partner, that also operates in the thought visionary realm in the food industry.

The success of this new-age wave of shopping has created a paradigm shift for other prominent retailers like Walmart, who have joined the culture of online shopping or even for chains retailers, such as grocery stores, that now offer online shopping and curbside pickup. Consequently, walking in a grocery store and immediately turning right is due to massaging thoughts with indirect influence, but ordering grocery online, in-home delivery, and picking it up at the curbside stem from thought leadership. The disruption in the status quo is not about influencing a customer's actions in a store, but creating a new mindset, where going in is no longer necessary.

Part II
FROM TRADITIONAL APPROACHES TO SELECTIVE CHANGE

CHAPTER 3

From Traditional Approaches to Selective Change

Every now and then a man's mind is stretched by a new idea or sensation, and never shrinks back to its former dimensions."

Oliver Wendell Holmes, Sr.

As indicated earlier, a central theme in this book focuses on selective change, meaning that organizational leaders and members opting to use internal cohorts to emphasize thought leadership will need to shift the way some processes are handled. One way to approach selective change is to review current practices to determine which practices will be restructured that will engage members in participative leadership. This is a critical step since most organizations follow a traditional approach of top-down leadership practices where the term "leader" refers to individuals in formal authority roles.

Traditional Leaders and Leadership Practices

Familiar statements such as "He's a natural born leader." or "She is destined to be a leader." fuel the ongoing nature vs nurture debate about whether leaders are born or developed by nurturing certain skills. At least one side of the argument was supported more than twenty-five hundred years ago by Confucius, who said, "To become a leader, you must first become a human being." It's difficult to debate his point of view. Other views propose that every leader must first be a follower; that every leader shifts positions from leader to follower based on situations and vice versa; but all views agree that regardless of personal traits, or technical skills, a leader must be developed. In either case, the term leader is usually defined based on specific traits of individuals that set them apart from non-leaders.

One comprehensive review of leader traits studies was conducted by Stogdill from 1904 to 1948, who reviewed 124 trait studies and later, 163 trait studies from 1949 to 1970. Findings from the studies indicated contributing factors that are relevant traits of leaders. Specific traits identified included intelligence, alertness to the need of others, task-oriented, self-confidence, initiative and persistence in dealing with problems, dominance and control, charisma and persuasive demeanor.

Table 1.1 Early Research on Leader Traits and Skills	
Traits	*Skills*
Adaptable to situations	Clever (intelligent)
Alert to social environment	Conceptually skilled
Ambitions, achievement oriented	Creative
Assertive	Diplomatic and tactful
Cooperative	Fluent in speaking
Decisive	Knowledgeable about the work
Dependable	Organized (administrative ability)
Dominent (power motivation)	Persuasive
Energetic (high activity level)	Socially skilled
Persistemt	
Self-confident	
Tolerant of stress	
Willing to assume responsibility	

R.M. Stogdill, Handbook of Leadership: A Survey of the Literature (New York:Free Press 1974)

Although, these traits are common among leaders, they are inconsistent in some areas since leader traits vary depending on power and influence or how the leader exercises power as relevant to the interests and needs of followers. This is especially true when the concept of leader is viewed based on circumstances outside of structured organizations and fragmented traits that exist in leaders across environments. Stogdill (1974) supports this notion and concluded:

> A person does not become a leader by virtue of the possession of some combination of traits...the personal characteristics of the leader must bear some relevant relationship to the characteristics, activities and goals of the followers.

In other words, there is no consistency or evidence of universal leadership traits, especially in determining how a leader is developed. Leader development may come from several sources. However, regardless, of development sources, there are certain observable traits that show a predisposition for leadership that occurs early in the behaviors and actions of youth.

An Early Predisposition for Leadership Exists

Scenario 2

A teacher in an early childhood center notices a pattern of several three-year-old boys in her class during free play. Each day when free play is announced, one boy says, "It's race time" and moves with several peers to the car station area. Once they get to the car play area, the boy who led the group to the area, passes out race cars to his peers. The teacher notices that over three days, the same boy selects a car for each peer, which is followed by several swift races around the rug track.

17

Winners of the race change each day, but the distribution of cars remains the same. After watching the behavior for four days, she decides to replace the cars in the storage bin with blocks but chooses not to tell the boys about the change. On the fifth day, the boys follow the same pattern. Once the announcer discovers that the cars are no longer there, he suggests, "Let's build towers" and begins the process of passing out several blocks to peers, who all wait their turn. Once the boys begin construction of towers, they take turns going to the storage bin to retrieve additional blocks as they strive to build the highest tower. The following week, the group returns to the same area and the teacher is amazed that peers wait for distribution of blocks by the same leading peer. During this exchange, one boy leaves the group and joins another group. The following day she returns cars to the bin and notice that the pattern of behavior continues.

The teacher makes an anecdotal note on her peer-interaction log, indicating that the group of boys uses an organized structure during free play and identifies the distributing child as a leader.

This case provides a compelling example in the prominent nature versus nurture argument about the origin of leaders. It demonstrates that leader development operates much like a funnel, where input determines output. Using the "funnel effect" as an analogy, leader development can occur from a supportive approach or survival approach. These terms support the notion that leaders are born with certain predisposition traits for leadership, but nurturing is necessary to enhance the tendencies.

In the supportive approach to leader development, early leadership traits, such as those demonstrated by this 3-year old, are nurtured by parents, teachers, coaches and peers, who encourage participation in opportunities that foster leader development. In this case, the funnel is filled with supportive strategies and opportunities for development by engaging a target child in opportunities to develop and apply leadership skills. As the child grows, verbal reminders (Be a leader; You are a leader, not a follower) are also provided to nudge thoughts that the child is a leader. These verbal reminders and influences of experiential learning opportunities have a great impact of leadership development.

Figure 1.1

Funnel Application of Leader Development

Supportive Development   Situational Development

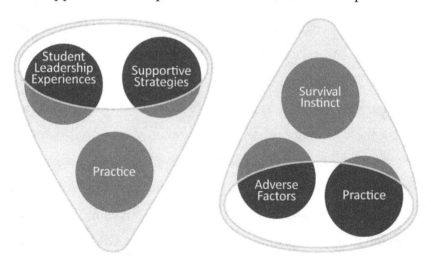

Student leader traits are recognized by adults and support is given to develop leadership skills | Student leader traits are ignored, but student develop leadership skills to improve life.

On the other hand, there are cases where the funnel is flipped, and individuals become self-appointed leaders. In this case, youth demonstrate early leader traits but there is a lack of supporting opportunities by adults for leadership development. Charisma becomes a key factor in leadership development, based on a set of personal behaviors. Max Weber brought this idea into the realm of leadership in 1947. He used 'charisma' to talk about self-appointed leaders who are followed by those in distress. Charisma, attributed to personality traits becomes the essence of persuasiveness. As an example, a child may experience early economic or social hardships, or other issues, and although unfair, adults may minimize strategies that support leadership development. Instead, the focus of adults is placed on providing essential tools for survival, with limited concerns about leadership. There are limited supportive strategies or opportunities to embellish leadership competencies, so the child personality develops based on efforts to overcome hardships and related factors. While some children take a passive role and endure, others use hardships as the driving force for change by seizing opportunities to assume leadership roles. Often these roles are related to maintaining core social elements for survival, fitting in with peers, concealing learning deficiencies or emotional stressors, which are coupled with proclivities to lead. Assuming certain roles forces propensities for leadership through the small opening in the flipped funnel. Once these forced inclinations begin to fill the funnel, many ooze out in the form of leadership competencies. The addition of charisma expands opportunities to persuade followers, resulting in an emerging leader. Self-appointed or self-developed leaders use charisma and tenacity to form relational bonds and followership that lead to significance influence in personal, social and business interactions.

In both cases, development is imminent, but conditions and attributes of leadership, especially charisma vary, leading to positive or negative leadership behaviors. Take a moment to reflect on peers that you grew up with. Which peers showed early leadership traits, but were intentionally or unintentionally ignored by adults based on circumstantial factors rather than their propensity for leadership? Who received attention and what was the criteria for supportive leadership strategies and coaching by adults? What happened to many of those peers in either case? Which category did your fall into? Are you considered a leader now? If yes, what were the greatest contributions to your development as a leader?

Whether early support is rendered or not, the truth is that it does not matter, which door leaders comes through, they all end up in the same room, because leaders are determined by followers. Consequently, how leaders arrive in the room called "leadership" is not as important as how they respond when they get there. The world is certainly filled with all types of leaders, who are nurtured along or self-made from circumstances. Since personality is a great determining factor in leadership quality, some children grow to become great leaders and other do not. In either case, leader development does not occur without followers.

Dynamics of Traditional Leader-Follower Roles

Another prevailing element of leader development comes from misdirected notions of adults, who lack a true understanding of leader-follower dynamics. Too often, parents, teachers and other adults posed the question to children, "Are you a leader or a follower?" The subtle implication behind these questions has always been "Be a leader, not a follower". These statements do not take in consideration that the role of leader is often temporary or situational based on the influence of followers. This is especially true for youth, when circumstances have a great impact on who will act as leader or follower. Although many children exhibit early traits of leadership, consistency in the use of those traits may be difficult with peers due to ongoing interests in popularity and attempts to fit in. Parents, teachers, coaches and other adults should keep in mind that leaders can only exist with followers and all individuals are required to shift roles throughout life. Consequently, questions should focus on how an individual's thoughts are being shaped in either role.

If we consider the magnitude of encounters and relationships required in our daily existence, it becomes difficult to imagine a world where everyone is a leader, because if everyone is leading, then the question becomes, who is following?

Whether intentional or unintentional, when leaders are paired with followers, two terms emerge - "leadership" and 'follower-ship." However, historically, the two terms have not received equitable significance. Massive volumes of books, lectures and training series have been written on leader development, and leadership, but research that focuses on followership indicates that followers are just as important, since a leader cannot exist without one or more followers.

Although leadership-followership roles vary in situations, the most familiar roles are seen in models that emerged in organizations where the relationship between leader and follower is based on status ranking between superiors and subordinates. Power and influence are two fundamental aspects of leadership in structured environments and are typically driven by leadership style. Historically, power has been the driving force behind how followers responded in their roles. Followers who had less influence, power and authority were less likely to voice their opinion or question leaders. In structured organizations followers depended on leaders for information and tended to act as bystanders and often silent supporters even in situations where leaders display horrendous behavior based on societal social standards. This is even a greater issue in a new society where fingertip access to information is prevalent. Communication in traditional and social media outlets, sway thoughts in so many directions increasing followership in a world where terms such as "going viral" influences thoughts and actions in many cases.

Today, a world of interwoven activities makes it increasingly difficult to avoid being a follower of some level of leadership at some point. However, being a follower is not a permanent assignment in the workplace. Questioning the views, actions and decisions of leaders can also serve as stimuli and motivation for change and open the gateway for individuals to think-outside-the box and disrupt the status quo. Consequently, new thought leaders emerge based on survival in a crowded marketplace as they recognize the need to create a shift in how things are done. Today, traditional leadership practices continue to exist, leadership doors are also forced opened in a nontraditional manner when new ideas emerge that demand recognition. More and more, people are seeking, discovering and taking advantage of alternatives ways of approaching and achieving results, creating the possibility for selective change in how personal and business matters are managed. It is this new discovery that creates a platform of thought leadership and its influence on organizational practices. Thought leadership creates a space that embodies opportunities for thought centered on alternative ways of doing things, where the so-called norm is challenged. Participation in this space offers engagement for selective change and authentic discussions about real time issues. Ideas about change and moving forward are met with anticipation, recognizing that today's followers can emerge as tomorrow's leaders.

An Analogy of Selective Change

Scenario 3

A young couple decides to purchase a new home to accommodate their growing family. As they begin a search for a new space, so many thoughts flood their minds as they remember that this is their first home together but also consider the reasons why the change is necessary. Throughout the process of searching for a new home, they think about favorite nuances in their present home that make them comfortable and how many of these things could never be reproduced. While there are essential items that they will hang on to, they realize that moving means adapting to a new environment and getting rid of familiar items that were once a part of everyday experiences. There are some things to throw away, give away, or sell. They ponder questions about what they are giving up and what they will gain. Will they lose a basement, but gain a two-car garage? What about the fun times in the basement with friends?

Is a basement a necessity in the new home? As they prepare for change, it will be necessary to avoid confusing the value of emotions and memories of former parties in the basement with the requirements for new spaces to accommodate current needs. After months of searching, they find a space, and both agree that it is the best choice for current and future needs. On moving day, they look around before the moving truck arrives and realize it is time to let go of the old and welcome the new. Sad thoughts prevail as the wife's eyes fills with tears, but the husband reminds her that in twenty-four hours this day will be over. The time has come to load the truck and move. After all, moving forward to a new home is happening based on selective change. This new move will not erase old sentiments and memories of days gone by, but it will open the door to new possibilities.

Like the realization of the young couple, approaching selective change in how things are done in an organization comes with recognition that old ways of doing things may disappear, but it also brings about the possibility of new ideas. Here again, a central idea of "disrupting the status quo" is prevalent. This proposition was emphasized in the fascinating book, Who Moved My Cheese, by Dr. Spencer Johnson. In his metaphorical analysis of change, Dr. Johnson, an internationally respected thought leader, emphasizes that change, whether forced or selective does not need to be the end, but rather an opportunity for a new beginning. Those relating his story conclude that, "change works best when everyone knows the story -whether it is a large organization, a small business, or a family - because an organization can only change when enough people in it change."

Questions to Consider:

1. *What pressing thoughts are prevalent regarding change in your organization?*

2. *How does change normally occur in your organization?*

3. *Which recent changes have been selective? Which ones have been forced?*

4. *How have organizational members or stakeholders responded to change?*

5. *What has been done to address concerns about change?*

6. *How has the organization benefitted from change?*

Part III
SHIFTING PERSPECTIVES ABOUT LEADERSHIP

Chapter 4

Seeing Differently

"No problem can be solved from the same level of consciousness that created it." - Albert Einstein

There is no doubt that our thoughts about most everyday tasks and interactions have been reshaped in a world, evaded by the immense explosion of technology. Changes are evident in almost every aspect of our lives, shifting thoughts about the things we do and the processes we use in daily activities. Our vehicles are connected to communication devices…we speak to gadgets to take care of routines in the home instead of family members…we shop for groceries, services and goods from the convenience of home. We live in a wireless society, but we are always plugged in. Adults and children are glued to captivating screens, which in many cases determine values and make sense of the world. Still, every day we are faced with new challenges to confront, and problems to be solved - better and faster. So, in an every-changing world, it is important to disrupt our routine thinking and train brains to think creatively about the things that matter.

Disrupting routine thinking involves seeing things differently from a new level of consciousness and looking for ideas that stray from traditional patterns. Seeing differently also means allowing our minds to think-out-side-of the proverbial box, offering the opportunity to peek into the rapidly- increasing territory of thought leaders.

The customary description of a "thought leader" generally refers to an individual with three distinguishing traits. First, the

29

individual is one with expertise in some specific area of special-ization. Second, the individual comes up with a distinctive idea and builds a following around, and third, the individual usually gains significantly profits from their ideas and is recognized as a thought leader.

However, the elements in this definition for thought leaders are not transferable as a conclusive definition for thought leadership and fail to include the latest research and scholarship on thought leadership. Research suggests that leaders require much more than technical expertise for effective leadership. Thought leaders are much more than individuals who present provoking ideas or valid scientific ideas, and observations rooted in their expert knowledge. They are individuals who are not only innovators but are self-motivators who reach and inspire other people. This trait is evident based on 2018 data from Forbes 400, noting that the origin of wealth for the richest Americans has shifted from inheritance sources to self-made individuals over the past 30 years.

Motivating others by determining "who's in" and building a following around an idea is a common thread that links all thought leaders, regardless of technical skills. A thought leader creates pathway that leads others to think. They have a strong propensity for nudging a thought along by first inspiring others, assessing the practicality of the idea, gaining technical support as needed, and utilizing an effective marketing strategy.

Inspiring others with ideas that disrupt the status quo requires personal traits beyond technical skills. Nurturing relationships and social networks, asking great questions of others and synthesizing that information into "actionable steps" envelope the constructs of thought leadership.

Simon Sinek's work - including his book, Start with Why: How Great Leaders Inspire Everyone to Take Action - delineates how thought leaders ask visionary questions and promote dialogue around core values, in addition to having the requisite technical skills to perform their roles. When these traits are considered in the definition of thought leadership, more impactful leadership roles can lead to shifts in how individuals or organizations improve interactions and productivity with knowledge through collaboration, and visionary thinking. Having a more inclusive definition of thought leadership offers the opportunity to recognize and include more individuals who embody diverse cognitive, emotional and social skills as well as experiences. Inspiring individuals, who are willing to collaborate about thoughts can enhance personal growth, positive shifts, and successful outcomes in organizations who now compete in an increasingly complex world.

Whether it's an aspiring youth, start-up entrepreneur, a corporate executive, public servant, servant leader or a non-profit leader, success is often dependent upon the ability to influence and engage others in getting on board with proposed ideas. Getting the message out and convincing others is an arduous task in a finger-tip controlled world flooded with millions proposing and launching the next big idea. Millions of face-to-face, electronic, and written daily exchanges of ideas create a crowded space for leaders attempting to showcase a distinctive breakthrough idea.

31

According to statistics, there are between 600,000 and 1,000,000 books published in the United States each year. These figures include thousands of self-published and how-to books and likely do not include ideas proposed by countless individuals seeking to share their latest inkling. In a world where thoughts run freely, the next great breakthrough idea can come from anyone, but the next great idea can also get lost or fail in a crowded marketplace, so it is critical that appropriate systems are in place to sustain forward-movement of the big idea.

Once an idea is organized in a systematic approach, the next step is to keep pushing forward knowing that there is always the possibility that the idea could very well be a hunch that disrupts the status quo. The key word here is possibility, since great ideas come without guarantees, and can easily fizzle out. Yet, the great news is that no one can predict that next person or what the next big idea will be, but we can predict that if the idea is cultivated properly, there will be a following around it. Thought leaders have certainly proven this to be true.

Chapter 5

Doing it Differently

Great leadership usually starts with a willing heart, a positive attitude, and a desire to make a difference - Mac Anderson

In recent decades, the idea of using thought leadership as a strategy has intensified as organizations look for approaches to remain competitive in crowded markets or stand out as a premiere entity setting standards for competitors to follow. This trend has also become widespread as more and more creative minds are taking advantage of technological innovations and emerging as a new breed of leaders.

Traditional Leaders

Traditionally, when we think of the terms "leader" or "leadership" in organizations, there is a typical assumption which implies reference to individuals who serve in the top-tier roles. Mental models of the terms leader and leadership tend to focus on formal roles associated with perceived abilities, power and hierarchy of management in organizations. A general definition of "leader" refers to a person who guides, rules or inspires others to follow and there is evidence that the person has one or more followers. Because of this broad definition, leaders are everywhere and come with numerous descriptions and perspectives about their development.

However, the term "leadership" is difficult to harness in one definition. It has been defined in terms of traits, behaviors, influence, interaction patterns, role relationships and occupation of an administrative position. After considerable review, Stodgill, (1974) concluded that "there are almost as many definitions of

33

leadership as there are persons who have attempted to define the concept". "Most definitions of leadership reflect the assumption that involves a process where intentional influence is exerted over others to structure, guide and assist activities and relationships in a group", (Yukl, 2010, pp. 2-3). This process of intentional influence is aligned with definitions of leadership that focus on paradigms of leadership roles that involve the process of giving purpose or meaningful directions to collective effort and the willingness to expend effort to achieve a specific purpose. Similarly, defining thought leadership is an arduous task, but it essentially focuses on influencing others.

Leadership is also about articulating visions, representing values, and creating an environment within which things can be accomplished. There are many examples of individuals who accomplish these conditions and are identified as leaders with no attachment to a formal organizational structure. In this case the definition of leader is viewed from a common lens involving a process whereby intentional influence is exerted by one person (a leader) to get other people (followers) to understand and agree about a specific idea or plan. Thus, the primary role of the leader is to influence actions and guide followers about what needs to be done, how to do it, and identify processes or procedures to accomplish shared objectives.

Thought Leaders

Similar elements exist in thought leadership where a leader engages others to build a following around a grand idea. But thought leadership is much more. It is about sharing insights and ideas - and a unique point of view - that provokes new ways of thinking, sparks discussions and debates, and inspires action. A true thought leader knows a topic inside and out, has formed a clear, unique and defensible point of view about it, and freely shares that perspective.

To better understand the magnitude of thought leadership, where ever you are right now, stop, look around, and examine the intricate details of a few things. Now scan your life and think of all the stuff you have, where it came from, why you selected it, and the difference it would make if it suddenly disappeared? Everyone knows that we live in a world of stuff, but our stuff did not appear as a poof from some magical cloud, it all came from a thought...that became an idea... that became a possibility... that became a process... and finally ... a reality. Now pick one item and ask yourself, how did the thought, idea, possibility, process and reality of this item flow? There are individuals noted throughout history for taking chances, experimenting, creating, developing and changing how individuals go about their daily lives. At one-time terms, such as inventor, innovator or trailblazers were descriptive terms to identify individuals who created major shifts in thoughts and processes. Now, the term thought leader, encompasses that level of productivity, when a mind shift occurs because of the idea.

Thought leaders come in many forms, without any special background or special genius but they are different and achieve success because they have learned how to put disparate elements together. They are noted experts, the leaders that others seek out, the ones who reshape the way we think, what we use, and how we use it. Thought leaders provide solutions and find interesting ways to influence others to buy-in to their ideas. However, being in a prominent leadership role is not a requirement for thought leaders. Five compelling traits set thought leaders apart from their counterparts:

- *how they think* ━━▶ *visionary*
- *the actions they take* ━━▶ *strategic - moves ideas along*
- *the ability to influence others* ━━▶ *inspires broader possibilities*
- *the results they achieve* ━━▶ *problem solvers*
- *the difference their ideas* ━━▶ *make shifts in society's beliefs*

Regardless of career status, notoriety or background, they present ideas in a new and meaningful way that captures attention. They say something or do something that disrupts thinking. These distinctions set individuals apart as thought leaders and serve as the threshold of "thought leadership". According to Dorie Clark, notable marketing and strategy consultant, thought leaders strive to make an impact, which requires them to get outside the ivory tower and ensure that their message is accessible and actionable.

Creating accessibility and actionable steps requires leadership. Whether small or big, ideas require attention, clarity for movement and may lead people in unexpected, contrarian directions. Given these factors, moving an idea from a simple thought to an explosive realistic format that secures a massive following and mind shift can be led by an individual. However, the decision to do things a different way involves more than a thought leader. It requires consensus building around an idea, which involves the use of a supporting team.

Doing it differently allows breakthrough ideas to extend far beyond the bounds of the developing organization. Once ideas are accessible, they become beneficial for competitors as well, based on the "bandwagon effect". The term derived from the figurative phrase, "hopping on the bandwagon", which entails following what others are doing. As an example, thought leadership at Southwest Airlines created a change in the flight industry regarding inflight food service by serving snacks on domestic flights for coach-class customers. Suddenly, peanuts, cookies, and a beverage of choice replaced small meals and became a common practice as an inflight food choice in coach class because other airlines bought into the idea. The option of purchasing food for coach-class, remains available, but primarily on international flights. Imagine the financial savings for Southwest's competitors because of the big idea from their thought leadership. Also, imagine the increase of sales for airport food vendors due to a shift in the mindset of passengers about the need to purchase a pre-boarding meal.

Thought leaders are trendsetters, in that they create a mind shift or change of focus and perception, but every trend does not emerge from a thought leader or meet the litmus test of thought leadership. For example, someone who starts a new fashion, style, etc., or helps to make it popular does not create a shift in mindsets about wearing clothes, but simply adds variety to wardrobe choices.

This is difference in cases such as Steve Jobs, Jeff Bezos, or Mark Zuckerberg where the magnitude of being trendsetter is significantly greater.

These examples illustrate a key trait of thought leaders, which is the ability to set themselves apart. They maneuvered their way to the top with significant influence that shifted perception and the way people respond in new trends by amassing substantial followers. Consider the phenomenon of social media. The first recognizable social media site, Six Degrees, was created in 1997. It enabled users to upload a profile and make friends with other users. In 1999, the first blogging sites became popular, creating a social media sensation that's still popular today. Seven years later, Mark Zuckerberg launched "The Facebook" in 2004, as it was originally known, later called Facebook in 2005, which now has 1.74 billion mobile active users (Mobile Facebook MAU) as of December 2016, which is an increase of 21% year-over-one year (Source: Facebook as of 02/01/17). What sets Zuckerberg apart as a thought leader is not development of the big idea called social media, but his influence in the industry.

The primary difference between a thought leaders and others in their industry is the preparation, planning and strategy that moves their idea to a level with significant influence where actions, interactions, and behaviors take on a different and recognizable approach. When thinking of thought leaders as influencers, the old phrase; "You can take a horse to water, but you can't make him drink", comes to mind. Thought leaders don't just bring the horse to the water, they convince him to drink day after day.

"Thought leadership is not about being known, it is about being known for making a difference." - Denise Brousseau

Questions to Consider:

1. *What traits set thought leaders apart from traditional leaders?*

2. *Do you have a strong knowledge base in a specific area?*

3. *How are you setting yourself apart from others in your industry?*

Part IV

LEVERAGING THE CONCEPT OF THOUGHT LEADERSHIP IN ORGANIZATIONS

Chapter 6

Leveraging the Concept of Thought Leadership in Organizations

"No one can whistle a symphony. It takes a whole orchestra to play it." - H.E. Luccock

When it comes to change in organizations, members tend to resist and set up barriers for many reasons. Sometimes resistance is due to personal fears or concerns, but barriers are also set up because of concerns related to leadership practices. In this case, the mindset of people may relate to ideas that reflect trust of leaders and what is viewed as priorities in leadership practices. Traditional mental models of leadership as a top-down structure, show that members respond to leaders based on formal role assignments within the organization. In these cases, leadership is comprised of one or a few individuals who follow a chain of command in a one-to-many tiered structure.

However, there are many compelling reasons to move beyond working with a single thought leader. For one, harnessing multiple voices as developers of ideas can exponentially increase the depth of an organization's team. Second, utilizing diverse thinkers leverages internal human capital resources to broaden the scope of ideas and will likely enhance creativity and ultimately set the organization apart as a unique entity in a business sector. The use of this approach provides an opportunity for enhancing participative leadership, giving a voice to members who are not in top-tiered leadership assignment roles.

Participative leadership also broadens the scope to support ideas of a thought leader as well as succession planning for leadership in case the primary thought leader leaves the organization. Another benefit of utilizing thought leadership as an internal strategy comes from the value of inclusionary practices. This is plausible as a platform in change initiatives since value is placed on getting perspectives from diverse members in the organization. Inclusion of diverse members in an organization provides a deeper probing centered around proposed change initiatives and increases influence on others. For one, colleagues working side-by-side have a vested interest in change that impacts their daily work environment and are more likely to engage when buy-in to change affects them directly.

Embracing thought diversity can also open the door for new innovative, unique ideas that can make a significant difference. One reason is that the use of members in leadership allows scaling of leadership development, which is more cost-efficient than the cost of formal leadership development programs. This would assist small companies or non-profit organizations, that are confronted with dwindling funding sources. The chart below identifies other areas where the use of internal thought leadership cohorts can benefit organizations.

What Internal Thought Leaders Can Influence

- *The priority of issues to tackle*
- *The choice of objectives and strategies to pursue*
- *The motivation of members to achieve the objectives*
- *The shared beliefs and values of members*

- *The influence of peers and colleagues to buy-in*
- *The development of new skills and confidence*
- *The learning of new information and sharing of new knowledge*
- *The enhancement of cooperation and mutual trust among members*

The idea of expanding participation in leadership activities beyond top-end leader roles is also supported in perspectives that view leveraging internal resources to build necessary in supporting frameworks of leadership. The Handbook of Leadership Development offers a supporting example of this new perspective, identifying Direction, Alignment, and Commitment (DAC) as three essential components of leadership (Wakefield & Bunker, 2010). The essence of these three components include:

- *Determining a direction for the organization through shared understanding of where the collective is headed as related to the organization's vison, goals and objectives.*
- *Alignment of effective communication, coordination and collaboration within the collective body.*
- *Commitment demonstrated by individual members demonstrating pursuing organizational collective goals as priority above individual goals.*

In summary, when organizational leaders employ inclusion of active members and entrust individuals with constructing a platform to share thoughts, there is a clear, powerful message being sent that leaders value them as well as their insights, demands and role in assisting change. Consequently, that vote of confidence fosters a sense of belonging, enhances ownership as an organizational stakeholder and increases overall emotional investment. This is beneficial for individuals, who may feel empowered as well as organizations as growth strategy by doing things in a different manner, thus demonstrating that there are observable advantages to doing it differently.

Ask yourself:

1. *What is happening in my organizations that would benefit from doing some things in a different way?*
2. *What are some "what if" questions that can be used to create ideas about changing processes?*
3. *Who should I include to move change ideas along?*
4. *How might doing things differently enhance productivity, growth strategy and the bottom line for my organization?*

Chapter 7

What If…Why Not? -Provocative Questions in Thought Leadership

"No problem can withstand the assault of sustained thinking."

Voltaire

The Big Idea:

What if we create cohorts of diverse members within organizations and provide training focused on thought management to move ideas forward; and show how skills could be replicated as a growth strategy to enhance overall performance and organizational culture?

Our Big Idea proposes the use of internal cohorts as a strategy to enhance participative leadership to promote change initiatives, growth strategy, creativity, organizational culture, and performance enhancement. We refer to this internal platform as a Thought Leadership Academy, which serves as a way of doing things differently in many cases. Recent research and informational pools on leadership describe three essential qualities beyond technical expertise that support effective leadership - mindfulness, emotional intelligence, and strategic thinking. Leaders who employ these qualities recognize that mindfulness, emotional intelligence and strategic thinking encompass more than a compilation of personal attributes but also should include leveraging those qualities in others. This is critical when considering the use of thought leadership as an organizational strategy.

When used in organizations, thought leadership typically operates on a spectrum of three domains: Product Thought Leadership (focus is on trends, point of views, trends and the future) Industry Thought Leadership (focus is on how- to processes, best practices, strategy) and Organizational Thought Leadership (focus is on organizational culture, talent development, performance enhancement, etc.).

According to a 2014 Forbes article, thought leadership is a new corporate strategy for 21st century organizations. Contributing Forbes author, Glen Llopis, proposes that many 21st century corporations are continuing traditional practices of business growth and failing to value and/or understand the power of knowledge sharing. Llopis emphasized that corporations must now begin to assess, package and share their own best practices, knowledge-sets, case studies and highly skilled, and talented leaders to serve as value-added resources to fuel business growth.

Employing thought leadership as a growth strategy with internal cohorts begins with asking provocative questions that challenge current practices. Asking questions can help reinvent industries and significantly impact business models, the marketplace, employees, consumers and the workplace. Harnessing the "collective mind" in a self-focused society is a great challenge for current leaders, so the use of cohort as a strategy can also fuel opportunities for employee engagement, enhance creativity, and infuse excitement back into a workplace culture.

However, there are a few points to clarify when considering engagement of employee-driven thought leadership cohorts that will improve the likelihood of success. First, there are two goals in developing and utilizing this platform- to augment participatory leadership practices and - enhance development of learning organizations. Second, consensus-building around ideas is critical to avoid launching a hodge-podge of ideas. Third, this approach could improve the use of participative leadership and increase buy-in. The intention of thought leadership cohorts is on developing strategic plans and implementing ideas around specific issues, rather than focus on management of an organization. Finally, use of a participative cohort leadership is from the lens of inclusion, where input from diverse members builds capacity and increases value of internal human capital.

There is significant evidence to show that confidence grows with learning, learning produces competence and competence produces results. Peter Senge emphasizes this point in his book -The Fifth Discipline- noting that as the world becomes more interconnected, it is no longer sufficient to have one person learning for the organization.

"It's just not possible any longer to figure it out from the top and have everyone else following the orders of the grand strategist".

Peter Senge

The goal here is to offer an opportunity that encourages intentional inclusion of diverse organizational members, who can share ideas, create interest in new ideas, spark creativity thoughts about problem solving that support growth and change initiatives. The use of intentional inclusion in this manner could also create a paradigm shift in internal leader development. In other words, dismissing the typical nomenclature that characterizes "leader" and including a diverse group made up of low-key, understated organizational members, may significantly improve outcomes. Utilizing diverse thinkers also provides an opportunity for cross-pollination of sharing ideas by members since everyone views the organizations through different lens-making diversity of thought a pathway for a breakthrough.

Another premise in focusing on thought leadership in organizations promotes the notion that participants in the process may not be traditional organizational leaders in terms of position or power but may offer ideas that act as a catalyst for change. In this case, internal thought leaders work collaborative to:

- *Broaden the organization's capacity as a leader in its sector.*
- *Improve content marketing.*
- *Create internal buy-in to enhance organizational culture.*
- *Strategic planning and performance growth.*
- *Assessing internal issues and formulating strategic solutions*
- *Launch breakthrough ideas that sets the organization.*
- *Serve as a leadership development approach for succession planning or new leaders.*

Since ideas tend to be plentiful in most cases where groups are concerned, thought leadership serves as the idea marker that move thoughts forward into a framework of building a following around it. Thought leadership encompasses spending time flushing out an idea and determining if it is feasible or practical based on the timeframe for development and implementation, resources or the acumen of organizational leaders and managing teams. Also, because getting buy-in from others around an idea is the core driving force for acceptance of a new idea, a third essential question, asking, "Who's in" is essential in thought leadership. Exploring this question from our perspective takes two groups in consideration: Who's in in terms of who will be in the organization's thought leadership cohort and "Who's In" based on who will buy-in as followers. Answering these questions when considering thought leadership as a strategy for organizations was initiated by pondering several supporting questions. The following "what if" and "why not" questions facilitated a conceptual framework for development of a Thought Leadership Academy.

1. *What if organizations leaders and members look beyond the typical hierarchal approach to spark interest in change or launch new ideas?*

2. *Would the use of organizational members, who are not in top-tier management positions enhance member buy-in of ideas that could set the organization apart from competitors?*

3. *Could this approach of inclusive participative leadership apply to any organization?*

4. *What if we utilize research-based models and best practices to improve thought management, communication, goal setting, and organization of actionable steps around ideas?*

5. *What if we attached the name Thought Leadership Academy to our process of helping groups to activate interest in changed, discover, create, cultivate and codify ideas?*

6. *What if we attached the name Thought Leadership Academy, to our process of helping groups to activate interest in changed, discover discover, create, cultivate and codify ideas?*

7. *Is our concept of a Thought Leadership Academy an out-of-the-box idea that could be a feasible growth strategy for organizations?*

8. *What if we customize our approach to activate or facilitate change using virtual and site-based training platforms to accommodate strategic change in different sectors?*

Probing these questions brought another thought to mind, why not go with it and see. One thing that is known about thought leaders is that it is impossible to tell where the next one will come from, which means that looking in unusual places can have its benefits.

So, why not? Why not move from a traditional perspective of looking for answers from "those in charge" to a more inclusive practice, where collective ideas become the new standard as a change strategy. This concept fosters the practice of empowering members beyond organizational leaders to carry ideas forward, amplify messages, create new norms and enhance goal attainment? Imagine that, but thought leadership is more than simply imagining … an idea must move forward and that's exactly what we are proposing! So, if you are in, bring your ideas and Let's Go!

Part V

NAVIGATING THROUGH COLLECTIVE THOUGHT PROCESSES FOR CHANGE

Chapter 8

Who's In? – Putting The BIG IDEA Into Practice

Change will not come if we wait for some other person or some other time. We are the one we've been waiting for. We are the change we seek. -Barack Obama

As mentioned earlier, my investigation of seminal work on thought leadership revealed no specific procedural outline for developing or utilizing the concept in organizations. However, processes for thought engagement and thought management were continuous interwoven threads in how thought leaders function when moving ideas along. Consequently, this section begins with a disclosure and warning.

Disclosure: Our Big Idea focuses on some strategies that can be adapted into the framework of development and implementation of a Thought Leadership Academy when used as an organizational strategy. While we have intentional selected certain research-driven models and best practices to use in the process of the development and implementation of site-based Thought Leadership Cohorts, these processes are not intended to serve the sole requirements for thought leaderships or an organization's efforts to move an idea along. We offer strategies while recognizing that human thought processes may lead to shifts in how they respond in group interactions or their perception about leadership and their role in participative leadership models. We know that training in team building will be critical and that selected members for the cohort may not be a good fit and will likely require adjustments. However, we know that creative mindsets are a good way to approach change.

Warning!!!

"The greatest waste in America is failure to use the abilities of people."

W. Edwards Deming

Establishing a Thought Leadership Cohort

"Thoughts are a prerequisite for thought leadership" - Neal Bruce.

Our focus is to highlight models and processes that stimulate disruption in the status quo, motivate individuals to behave differently, enhance creativity, and develop opportunities to develop and try new ideas. Anyone familiar with leadership knows that there is well-documented evidence that the road to change is often paved with unpredicted potholes and ever-changing challenges on a craggy bumpy terrain. Yet, despite the challenges of daily interactions in organizations, leadership is about providing intentional influence for articulating visions, establishing goals, embodying values and creating productive environments where things can be accomplished. Given this formidable task, our perspective for the use of thought leadership can be applied to any sector because the idea focuses on enhancing collective engagement and capacity.

In business we are always passing from one significant moment to another significant moment, and the leader's task is pre-eminently to understand that moment of passing. The leader sees one situation melting into another and has learned the mastery of that moment (Follet, 1920, p. 120)

Is Follet's statement an ongoing reality in your organization? Do situations melt into another or clump together in certain areas, resulting in piles of uncertainty and clogged pathways to progress. Are you aware that daily moments and situations offer provoking opportunities for leaders and members to examine and rethink mental modes about how things are or wish them to be? With this thought in mind, recommended tools and strategies in this chapter are designed to help level the ride on the often tumultuous pathway to change and transition. Following principles and practices used in thought leadership provides a scaffolding approach to activate interest in change, develop creative systems to facilitate change, implement and sustain collective engagement, and subsequent capacity building around organizational change initiatives. These practices can be applied to either domain of thought leadership when the goal is to impact overall improvement.

Day-to-day structures in supporting the existence of organizations demonstrate a complicated process as more and more challenging demands confront leaders. One way that leaders are treading unforeseen waters is by embracing strategies that support inclusion of members through participative leadership. Integrating organizational members in leadership practices who are not serving in leadership roles requires careful mastering of a tapestry of woven threads bonded by individual and group priorities. The focus is gathering ideas through reflection, analysis, collaboration, diverse thoughts and proactiveness that support the vision and goals of the organization. Consequently, the use of internal teams is an ever-increasing leadership strategy, framed by the acknowledgment that "All of us are smarter than any one of us." However, this statement does not mean that leaders should arbitrarily select groups of individuals, without meticulous consideration of their ability to function as a group, utilize creative and innovative thought, build consensus around ideas and assist in the development of viable strategies that will promote and facilitate sustainment of new ideas. Accomplishment of these functions enhances team-effectiveness as well as sustainable outcomes.

Other characteristics of a group include the following collective covenants emphasized by Kozlowski and Ilgen (2006), who noted that group members (1) share a social identity as a unit; (2) share common goals; (3) have distinct roles as part of the team; (4) work interdependently to achieve goals, tasks and outcomes; and (5) are embedded in the broader organizational and societal context that they influence or are influenced by. These are key elements in our recommended use of thought leadership cohorts, since they should function by the standards identified based on an effective team's functioning approach.

However, following standards that impact team cohesiveness is not enough in a thought leadership cohort, it is also necessary to pay attention to leadership capabilities of the proposed individuals. Members should have unique traits, that will assist collective thought management and consensus building, so that decision-making can meet the litmus test of provocative thoughtful ideas. Strong consideration should also be given to enhancing diversity among members based on beliefs, values, creativity and expertise from experiential learning. Careful consideration should be given to personality traits and clear statements about the scope of leadership roles that the cohort will have. Formal training should be a factor, but not a sole indicator for selection or elimination. A key thought to keep in mind is that the lack of diversity may preclude potential outcomes especially in areas, such as creativity, innovation and shared equity for all members. Creativity as a selection factor is important since it is a contributing component in thought leadership. Ideas will fall apart if members lack essential knowledge, necessary skills, and experience aligned with targeted goals. Think about individual ideas, target areas or projects requiring change in your organization. Where is there a need to disrupt the status quo? Now consider internal change agents that won't just "go with the flow", but "who will also create the flow". So, who's in?

Questions to Consider:

Ask yourself...

1. *What defining qualities will cohort members need to be an effective component in our organization?*

2. *How will we define diversity in the cohort?*

3. *What initial standards should we uses as criteria for members?*

4. *How can we establish a framework that supports authentic thought, thought management, active engagement, confidentiality, effective communication and consensus building?*

5. *Who's in?*

Chapter 9

Let's Go! - Using Thought Leadership Cohorts as
a Strategy in Organizations

"Strategy is a pattern in a stream of decisions" - Henry Mintzberg

What thoughts come to mind, if someone says to you "Let's talk strategy"? Do you immediately ponder a number of ideas that might address the situation, play possible resolution scenarios in your head, wonder what might come next, or ask for more details to help generate ideas? A correct answer may be any or all the above depending on who's included in the discussion. The term, "strategy" is difficult to define since many people confuse and intertwine what it means with how it works. One great explanation on the term comes from the logic of a favorite cartoon character, Foghorn Leghorn, during one of his many wise mentoring moments with his young counterpart: "Listen here boy, I say... I say, we've got to do some thinking... and... we've got to do some doing". This is a practical description of strategy, as it encompasses some thinking as well as some specific actions to resolve or address a situation.

Words and phrases tantamount to strategy such as a plan, approach, line of attack, or tactic can be utilized as lens to view what happens when the term is applied to the need for actionable responses. Organizations utilize two types of strategy, which include business strategy and leadership strategy.

- *Business strategy - the pattern of choices an organization makes about the way things will be done, so that it can be viable in its sector or maintain a competitive advantage.*

- *Leadership strategy - describes the human capabilities in an organizational that are needed to maintain operations and perform activities in the business strategy.*

When aligning the concept of strategy with "thought leadership", both types are relevant. Strategy in this case is not a short-term or immediate response but employs tactical thinking to make choices about short-term and long-term direction, alignment with goals, and commitment to completion or fulfillment. The idea is to become more thoughtful about how to best accomplish a goal, while recognizing that being strategic in an organization can be challenging since it requires execution of ideas that could impact priorities for various segments of the organization. First, developing an appropriate strategy for a situation should yield results that benefit target groups, but more importantly the organization. The following scenario provides an issue that can serve as an example of how organizations need a business and leadership strategy to remain as a competitive entity.

Scenario 4

A restaurant near several major corporate multiplexes in a large city is known for its specialty breads and serves several types of sandwiches as featured items on its daily menu. Unlike franchise competitors in the area, the restaurant uses fresh bread that is baked daily on site for its sandwiches. Positive customer reviews about the fresh-baked unique flavored breads have set the restaurant apart from other sandwich shops in the area, causing a high volume of daily customers during lunch. Flour is delivered daily due to the volume of bread required and limited storage space. During the past month, the delivery truck has arrived 45 minutes to an hour later than normal delivery time, causing significant frustration for restaurant workers who are responsible for preparing bread. The delivery truck driver has informed the manager that roadwork in the area is causing traffic delays and construction will continue for several months. Alternate routes have longer traffic jams, since many drivers are using detours to avoid construction. The owner is concerned that he will lose customers if the quantity and quality of bread is unavailable during the lunch period due to a delay in getting the necessary ingredients. The owner informed the day manager that a meeting to develop a "strategy" is required to discuss options that will sustain their customers base.

This case reveals that organizational issues are often influenced by internal and external factors. It also shows that an influx of factors from either can cause trickle-down or subordinate issues to simultaneously come to the forefront, leaving leaders with the challenge of finding a strategy that taps into more than one area. When applying thought leadership to this scenario, leaders will foster ideas that will address the big problem, while also focusing on contributing sub-issues linked to short-term and long-term issues.

Consider these questions as starter prompts for planning a strategy: (1) Is bread or customer experience the greatest asset for the organization? (2) What are some issues other than flour delivery that are influencing the stability of the restaurant? (3) Should the frustration of workers (bakers) be a major concern when developing a strategy? (4) How might the frustration of workers impact the customer base? (5) Since the construction is a temporary matter, is it practical to look at a long-term solution or just focus on current issues? (6) How might all workers be included in selecting a strategy? (7) What practical long-term fixes can be applied to ensure a sustainable customer base? (8) How will ideas around the long-term fixes move forward?

This way of approaching strategy is reflected in our concept and use of thought leadership, where knowledge and ideas from a group take on a dual role. First, it coheres with leadership and work of management, and second, it supports alignment with ideas of people who work together for the whole rather than parts, which is a primary element of system-thinking.

In addition, the evolution of strategies can involve more than thoughts of top-tier leaders. Mintzberg (2011) in his book *Managing* emphasizes that strategies can emerge without being formulated in formalized planning sessions but can also emerge through efforts of formal and informal learning. Mintzberg notes that "Strategies are not tablets carved atop mountains, to be carried down for execution" (p.163). Leaders promoting thought leadership should utilize an engaging approach by allowing thousands of strategic flowers to bloom in their organizations. This is far more beneficial than spending long hours in a leadership hothouse carving out strategies. Like hot house fruit, strategies which emerge in this rushed manner may be viewed by users as lacking the quality flavoring of fruit that takes time to grow properly and is harvested in the appropriate season. The same is true for developing a cohort as a strategy. Development will take time to carefully examine potential cohort members and what role they will play as a participative leadership development. Specifically, the selection process should take several steps to determine criteria for potential participants.

Whether attempting to singularly or collectively move ideas along, several research-driven strategies can be used to assist individual or organizational efforts. These strategies can serve to formulate thoughts into frameworks that promote a scaffolding and synthesizing process around ideas. Research-driven models and best practices are beneficial because of proven results when identifying and codifying systems for weaving through ideas. However, keep in mind that these suggestions are used as an investigative approach of a thought leadership platform and are not intended as sole exclusive requirements for moving ideas along. Also, further development of awareness and experiential use of these recommended practices will enhance learning potential of cohort members and further practices of organization interested in building a learning-oriented culture. Use of the following strategies will achieve two goals; activate interest in change, facilitate change ideas and sustain change.

Strategy 1 – Employ the concept of system-thinking as a primary reason for considering organization change.

"System- thinking supports the need to triangulate. You need to get different people, from different points of view, who are seeing different parts of the system to come together and collectively start to see something that individually none of them see." - Peter Senge

Leadership is about the ability to grasp the total situation or looking at the whole (Follet, 1920). When organizing thoughts about what is best for the organization, leaders are required to see the whole, rather than a kaleidoscope of individual pieces. System thinking is a discipline for seeing the wholes (Senge, 2006). It looks for interrelated patterns rather than snapshots of separate parts. Think about a visual representation of a jigsaw puzzle on a box. The outside box top shows the outcome, but inside the box are many pieces that must fit together to complete the picture seen on the outside. System-thinking in thought leadership is about sorting the pieces, looking at distinguishing traits for each piece and linking the pieces together, one piece at a time.

System-thinking is especially relevant now because of the abundance and complexity of information that confronts us daily, creating a network of interlocking interdependence. Let's apply this framework to the issue at the restaurant of late delivery of flour. Issues arising from the external factor of roadwork have led to interlocking issues between the delivery company and the restaurant, impacting services by both companies. Leaders in this case must view the issue as a reality that is affecting the whole because in both cases, the breakdown of business has to do with customer experience, rather than individual products. If the delivery business fails to satisfy its customer, (the restaurant) and the restaurant fails to satisfy its customer (sandwich buyers) looking for that great taste experience at lunch, both companies lose. The primary concern now is the loss of customers during construction, but a greater concern is that the loss of customers can also be long-term if the quality of customer's experience falls short shifting thoughts to eating at other area restaurants.

Question to Consider:

1. *What issues at your organization can be benefit from a system thinking*

perspective help to create solve short-term and long-term solutions?

2. *How can system-thinking be utilized in shifting processes?*

Strategy 2- Use Cognitive Diversity in a Thought Leadership Cohort

"If you do not intentionally and deliberately include, you will unintentionally exclude."- Michael Fullan

What if your organization was recommended to participate in a competitive opportunity, where the winner would be the first organization to complete a six month experiential action learning project in outer space? Consider the following questions about planning for the competition and being the winner.

1. *Who is the first person in your organization that comes to mind for planning a winning strategy? Why?*
2. *Who would you recommend as a leader for the group and why?*
3. *What other members would you recommended to organize a winning strategy? What special skills will they offer?*
4. *What type of personal attributes would team members need?*
5. *Would you like to be on the competitive team? Why/Why not?*
6. *Who would you leave off the team? Why?*
7. *What major qualities of your organization should judges consider?*
8. *If your organization wins the competition, who should take the trip, team members, leaders or both?*
9. *How would you get organizational members to buy-in to the idea?*

These questions can be the starting point when developing any team for any purpose and could be a viable starting point for development of a thought leadership cohort. Employing cognitive diversity should be a strong consideration when developing a cohort focused on thought leadership. Creating a thought leadership cohort should follow the same principles used for developing any team. Consider, how teams develop in organized sports. Before a team plays, someone contemplates who will play on the team and what roles each member will play. Selection of members with diverse skill sets will greatly enhance varied approaches to reach desired outcomes. Development should be based on skill acumen, along with other attributes so that collective thoughts can produce a well-rounded narrative about ideas or interests. This can be accomplished when teams use cognitive diversity in the selection process.

Cognitive Diversity refers to the extent which a group demonstrate differences in knowledge, including beliefs, preferences and perspectives based on variations in how individuals process information. It is not predicted by factors such as gender, ethnicity, or age, but rather, how individuals think about problems, and engage with new, uncertain, and complex situations. However, cultural background is an important aspect of cognitive diversity since experiences influence how individuals react and respond. Our experiences determine our perceptions of situations.

Three Important Reasons for Using Cognitive Diversity in Thought Leadership

- *Inclusion of Baseline-Level Thinkers*

Use of diverse members can provoke thought at a baseline-level related to everyday internal functioning activities that may be viewed as nominal by top-tier leaders. This is especially true when trust is strained in terms of job security, work-loads and repeated intentional or unintentional exclusion of low-level organizational members based on hierarchical approaches to leadership.

Gathering diverse perspectives to address problems, issues and find solutions allows inclusion of members in processes that impact their daily interactions and experiences. This is important when approaching change in organizations, because making changes often requires going against the wind in social-centered environments. Think about colleagues that you interact with at work beyond employment responsibilities. Who do you eat lunch with or hang out with socially beyond the work day? These individuals probably share some common interests or perspectives because social relationships tend to be based on a mirroring-effect. People associate with others based on similarities reflecting how they see themselves. Aligning with others who have common interests and perspectives about the organization aids in creating subcultures.

• *Cognitive Diversity enables the inclusion of perspectives from subcultures.*

Subcultures in organizations often reflect the familiar quote of General George S. Patton, which says, "If everyone is thinking alike, then somebody isn't thinking." In other words, influence grounded in social interactions create subcultures in organizations that can impede or enhance change ideas.

• *Cognitive Diversity offers an opportunity to gather perspectives from different types of thinkers.*

Consideration for diverse perspectives encourages and engages individuals in revealing and deploying different modes of thinking as well as looking at or trying things in multiple ways. It's can

69

be described as "thinking differently-together". Here is where mindfulness and emotional intelligent become congruent with thought management about ideas that support change. When cognitive diversity is a key element of cohort development, a door is opened for individuals to be authentic. One major use of thought leadership is formulating processes that can move an idea along from conception to completion. To accomplish this goal, imagine the process of putting a jigsaw puzzle together where each piece is required to achieve the whole picture. Authentic thought allows an opportunity to utilize individuals with different thinking styles. Cognitive scientists have identified several ways to thinking or thinking styles, which can facilitate the development of ideas. These include:

- *Creative thinking - innovative "out-of-the-box" thinking where imaginative, disruptive thinking is used to assess and put together ideas, procedures, and possibilities. (These are the "what if"- why not" people).*

- *Analytical thinking - logical step-by-step organized thinking that breaks down processes by scaffolding procedures to reach the end. (Great problem-solving skills)*

- *Critical Thinking - involves the ability to use objectivity and good judgment in understanding what is happening and why. Focus is on arriving at answers as well as identifying influential factors that contributed to the conclusion. (Supports analytical thought and finding solutions).*

- *Abstract Thinking - style allows individuals to take ideas and make connections. Ability to find hidden meaning behind what is being said or observed. (These are creative people who look beyond reality and imagine something new.)*

- *Concrete Thinking - involves understanding and applying facts and details. Matter-of-fact on the surface thinking based on that which is precise or verbatim. (Great for finding literal meaning).*
- *Divergent Thinking - refers to the ability to generate ideas by exploring many different options and solutions to solve an issue prior to finding the most appropriate answers. Allows for creativity in searching for possible solutions. (Great for creating options).*
- *Convergent Thinking - involves the process of finding the single best, logical solution for a problem. Convergent relies more on logical frames than creativity in looking for a solution or answer. (Great for keeping on schedule and adhering to timelines).*
- *Sequential/Linear Thinking - step-by-step progression thinking. (These are the strategic thinkers, who are great for creating flow patterns or process mapping).*
- *Holistic/Nonlinear Thinking - the ability to see the big picture as well as how parts are interconnected to create the whole. Expanded thinking enables individuals to expand thoughts in different directions rather than maintaining a singular viewpoint. (These are the "big picture" people).*

In summary, cognitive diversity provides a more inclusive, collaborative and open space where people feel empowered to create and implement ideas. Intentional inclusion of varied styles of thinkers has its benefits, especially when supported by strategic implementation of processes that codify shared ideas. The idea of using cognitive diversity as a springboard in developing a thought leadership cohort can be summarized by thoughts from renown author and motivator, John Maxwell who has identified a formula for moving thoughts along: Maxwell's formula:

> *The Right Thought plus the Right People*
> *in the Right Environment at the Right Time*
> *for the Right Reason = Right Result*

Questions to Consider:

1. *What types of thinkers are needed to seamlessly move ideas in your organization?*

2. *Who would be ideal people at your organizational to include in a thought leadership cohort based on their personal thinking style?*

3. *If you are a sole entrepreneur or small company, how can the use of a support cohort serve as a growth strategy?*

Strategy 3 - Employ "Strength Finders" to discover individual strengths in groups.

> *"From the cradle to the cubicle, we devote more time to our shortcomings than to our strengths." - Tom Rath*

One thing most of us learn early in life is that there are some areas where we excel and some things that we just can't seem to do well. It's too bad that some do not discover early in life because it would save a lot of time for some aspiring musicians. Nevertheless, there is ample evidence to show that everyone's brain is uniquely wired, which enhances development of strengths in some area and limits other. The primary issue is that learning programs continuously devote inordinate time focusing on shortcomings in flawed attempts to find a balance between strengths and weaknesses, which is referred to as "the path of most resistance", (Rath, 2007).

In his book -Strength Finders, 2.0- Rath emphasizes that the aim of almost any learning program is to help individuals become who they are not. We have all heard someone say "you can be anything you want", when the truth is that some things require natural abilities and no one person is wired to do everything. Consequently, it's best to strive for being the best of what you can be. This stance will likely yield a better outcome as leaders seek to find individuals with the best talents to accomplish tasks related to their organization's vision and goals. Here the focus placed on a strengths'-based perspective, which recognizes that every individual is different, and job functions or processes require consideration for the best contribution that each person can offer.

Strength Finders is a fascinating tool that evolved from long-term research, initially led by the late Donald Clifton and a team of scientists at Gallup. For more than 75 years, Gallup studied behavior of children and adults in more than 150 countries, which led to the development of the Clifton Strength Finders Assessment. Research over 40 years focused on helping individuals discover and describe personal talents based on 34 markers of common talents. The assessment has been translated into more 20 languages, and is used by businesses, schools, and community groups.

Strength Finders 2.0, is an expanded version of the original work and will have strong implications as a tool in a thought leadership cohort for several reasons. One obvious reason is that launching ideas requires people with different skills and talents. Thought leaders don't become experts by accident, but they also are not skilled in every aspect of competencies needed to build sustainable systems around their idea. There are many processes that go on behind the scene that moves an idea along. Applying Strength Finders in thought leadership will help members identify personal strengths so that task assignments for projects can be made based on strengths. Gallup has surveyed more than 10 million people worldwide on employment engagement (how positive and productive people are at work), which makes the Strength Finders assessment a viable tool for identifying an individual's strength. Information gathered in this massive research indicates that capitalizing on strengths in organizations can accentuate goals and efforts, especially when individual strengths are included in planning. Another benefit of using the tool early in development of the cohort is that personal strengths tend to drive interests and efforts, which can serve as an advantage when diverse skills are needed to create and build ideas. Since thought leadership serves to create or move ideas along, a discovering strengths of cohort members will be a great value to ensure the possibility of a productive group that can accomplish desired outcomes.

Questions for Reflection:

1. *What steps can we take early to harness individual strengths of cohort members to solve problems and enhance productivity?*

2. *What strengths do you bring to a group or organizations that will benefit progression of ideas?*

Strategy 4 - Allow adequate time to develop a cohesive Thought Leadership Cohort

Coming together is a beginning. Keeping together is progress. Working together is success. - Henry Ford

Most descriptions of thought leaders refer to individuals with expertise in a specific sector, who are the go-to individuals in that area. However, regardless of expertise, thought leaders need help.

Whether a new innovative idea or change in mindset, it is difficult to imagine that a thought leader is productive in moving an idea along in isolation. This is apparent in an interdependent society, where innovative thoughts require processes that include others to weave through the complexity of launching ideas. One indicator of this process is highlighted by the popular show "Shark Tank", which provides a great lens for identifying individuals vying for recognition of being an innovator. Each week, individuals showcase their "big idea" on the auction stage hoping to capture the interest and financial support of tenacious self-made millionaires and billionaires with acute business expertise. Like the flip of a coin, some ideas are a winning toss, while others are not. However, regardless of successful wooing or failed attempts to acquire financial investment and marketing support, some continuing themes emerge from exercises in this investment chess game. First, the theme of creativity is obvious as entrepreneurs present their big idea. Second, it is obvious that while creativity is a starting point for big ideas, having a strong knowledge in product development, growth strategy and astute aptitude in financial management are determining links for buy-in to big ideas by the Sharks. It is evident that there is need for a team to move ideas along.

Shark Tank also illustrates that what constitutes a great idea is relative to who is reviewing it, which may limit possibilities for launching and more importantly sustaining an idea for profitable gain. If application of these principles is used in business, then the benefit of collective thought around ideas will enhance viability, fidelity, and sustainability. However, gathering a team of individuals together also involves the realization that the "human factor" will impact processes. So, developing team-building skills will be a priority. Information regarding team-building is immense, but many resources identify creating teams that will... (1) share a social identity as one unit, (2) share common goals, (3) work interdependently to complete tasks (4) have distinctive roles in the group, (5) focus is on achieving successful outcomes that affect a greater group or good than individual goals. Since a primary objective of an organizational thought leadership cohort is to assist in building a" learning organization" it is essential that time is allocated for assessing group dynamics, training, and coaching to build competencies in leadership as well as effective team functioning. Consequently, allowing time for development of a well-rounded thought leadership cohort will improve chances for collective thought and consensus building to generate and build mechanisms to codify ideas.

Questions to Consider: Ask yourself...

1. *What internal and external support or resources are required to develop effective team competencies necessary for a productive cohort?*

2. *How can you contribute as a viable member of a cohort in your organization?*

Strategy 5 – Use Appreciative Inquiry (AI) as a process to clarify specific target areas that the cohort will address.

"Commitment without understanding is a liability" - Oliver Wight

How would you respond to a friend, who stops by your office and ask you to accompany him on a trip, but could not provide any clue about the destination? Apart from youngsters on a joy ride, this idea would probably be met with a lot of resistance. The same would be true if a colleague approached you about joining a work group without an awareness of why it was necessary or reason for selecting you. So far, we've offered discussions about creating a platform for idea development and implementation, but these actions are futile without a concentrated focus on identifying and prioritizing organizational needs and the role that the cohort will play in addressing those needs.

Like planning a trip, planning for a cohort should start with the end in mind by identifying target goals for the group. One end goal should be to get sustainable results - not just new processes. So, a first step would be to identify areas where results will be beneficial by allocating time for an explicit discovery of the organization's status. A great advantage of using Appreciative Inquiry is that it provides an opportunity for focused thinking, which narrows the scope of ideas and target areas of focus. Since cohorts operate in a participative leadership mode, steps in Appreciative Inquiry (AI) bring clarity to the role of the group and what that role will entail. It will also help establish priorities as well as dreams for new possibilities. Focused thinking is applied in two areas:

- *Appreciation – members recognize and value the contributions or attributes of things or people that are currently in place.*
- *Inquiry – members exploring and discovering, in the spirit of seeking to better understand, and being open to new possibilities.*

The Appreciative Inquiry Model serves as a basic roadmap for beginning transformational change through five questioning steps, or "D-Steps". The five steps focus on (1) Defining the focus of inquiry, (2) What is working best at the current time? (3) What might work, (4) Dreaming about how change will look, and (5) Designing and Delivering how change will be sustained. The use of Appreciative Inquiry reflects similarities to the change processes that eagles undergo in sustaining strength.

Eagles go through a molting process where they shed their old feathers and grow new ones. This process is necessary in the rejuvenation of the eagle, so it can continue to remain strong.

Cohort members will benefit from thorough training in Appreciative Inquiry to facilitate successful awareness of processes and how to engage in practical use of the model to understand benefits of a molting process in organizations.

Questions to Consider: Ask yourself...

1. *How can our cohort benefit from the use Appreciative Inquiry to initiate and drive ideas?*

2. *What brainstorm ideas come to mind for starting the process of developing a cohort?*

Strategy 6 – Practice gently asking provocative questions with "Humble Inquiry" and using nonjudgmental listening with "Active Inquiry".

"What we ask and the particular form in which we ask it is ultimately the basis for building trusting relationships, which facilitates better communication and, thereby, ensures collaboration where it is needed to get the job done." - Edgar Schein

Humble Inquiry

"Ask, don't tell" is not the most frequent phrase in business environments, because telling others what to do is an ongoing occurrence in traditional leadership and often serves as the territorial boundary between leaders and followers. Thought leadership offers an opportunity to intentionally shift this practice in some instances by engaging in "humble inquiry" (gentle asking-rather than telling) and active inquiry (questioning and non-judgmental listening). Both models of inquiry were outlined by Edgar Schein, a foremost thought leader in organizational culture. Each process serves to ease potentially anxiety-provoking revelations of individuals about authentic feelings and provide a scaffolding process for gathering essential information around an issue or ideas.

Humble Inquiry is process of asking provocative questions in a manner that influences people to tell the truth about what is going on. According to Schein (2009), there is compelling need for using "humble inquiry" as a practice to unveil authentic thoughts in discussions. Humble inquiry is skillfully asking questions that will draw out an individual's real feelings, gather authentic answers, build relationships to enhance discovery of solutions. In thought leadership, answers are not presented to discover abstract ideas, but to gather authentic answers about realistic day-to-day experiences.

Active Inquiry

Active Inquiry as a process focuses on nonjudgmental listening, which we refer to as fertile listening. The process act as a safe container in which it is possible for individuals to handle issues that may be too hot to handle under ordinary circumstances. This process of questioning opens the door for an individual to feel okay about authentically answering: "How does this relate to me-my priorities -my work"? Utilizing questioning processes and humble inquiry can also enhance Accountable Talk, which refers to the process of meaningful expressions that provides clarity for the speaker and listener during communication.

When these processes are used as thought leadership practices, guiding ideas or target change goals are aligned with real-life experiences and thoughts. Linking the two models allows opportunities for strategic application of Appreciative Inquiry where realistic answers are used when defining, discovering, dreaming and designing ideas about the organization. Development in the use of the three- models will serve as a great approach when developing systems for how information supporting ideas will be collected and shared.

Strategy 7- Create S.M.A.R.T.E.R. Goals

"A goal without a plan is just a dream." - Dave Ramsey

We all know that goals are important in life and are required to guide the pathway to accomplishing desired outcomes. With this mind, starting any plan requires assessing where you are as well as identifying where you are trying to go. Goals reflect both positions and serve as markers from start to finish. Best practices show that the use of S.M.A.R.T.E.R. Goals acts as an effective tool to identify touch points from start to finish for aspirations for individuals as well as organizations.

The term S.M.A.R.T.E.R. serves as a mnemonic acronym that represents an approach for developing and managing goals. Representative terms vary, but when applying the acronym in business frameworks, the term indicates that goals should be written as follows:

- *Specific - very specific, concise statement identifying the desired outcome.*

- *Meaningful - identifying process that can be measured, rather than generalizations. In business, the term "meaningful" is applied to reflect importance of desired outcomes to individuals as well as the organization.*

- *Achievable - Goals should be set based on the probability that they can be achieved. The intent is to develop a goal that makes sense in terms of rational outcomes, rather than "pie-in-the-sky". This does not mean that everything must be in place, but goals should reflect what might be possible.*

- *Relevant - In business goals should be relevant to the mission and core values of the organization. When setting goals to move ideas, there should be evidence of alignment with other frameworks within the business.*

- *Time-bound - A goal should identify a time-sensitive period for completion.*

- *Evaluate - Evaluation of goals is a key step in measuring progress as well as outcomes or achievement. Evaluating is an ongoing process so that changes to drive intended outcomes can be monitored.*

- *Readjust - The final step in setting goals to make readjustments as needed based on evaluation of processes. Readjustment does not mean throwing away a goal or removing a desired outcome, but rather making changes to improve the likelihood of achievement.*

Goal setting in thought leadership serve as an essential component to drive ideas forward and foster shared thinking. One reason is that ever-changing advancements require ongoing adjustments that address new challenges or systems.

Strategy 8: Use Project Design Models & Project Mapping to move ideas from concept to conversion.

"Our goals can only be reached through a vehicle of a plan, in which we must fervently believe and upon we must vigorously act. There is no other route to success." - Pablo Picasso

Thought leadership is no secret sauce that automatically gets an idea from conception to launch. In fact, development of ideas sometimes takes years as a thought leader and the supporting team work out details. Once an idea becomes the focal point for development, it will be necessary to identify a design model that will guide the project along as well as assist in the development of systems that will sustain it. This will be the most difficult phase of a project as cohort members build and stretch thoughts into actionable steps.

Businesses vary in numerous ways which lead to vast ideas and projects, so critical thought is required to determine the most appropriate project design model that will facilitate goal attainment and target outcomes. Thought leadership is about utilizing strategic processes that involve a cycle of continuous learning, testing, execution, analysis and repetition. There is an extensive list of process design models to guide basic and complex procedural cycles for idea development. Organizations should invest in training cohorts on methodologies that are structured, but adaptable to meet the target needs based on the project. Internal cohorts would Utilizing a structured design model also supports the concept of being a "learning organization" by introducing new concepts, modeling, testing and transferring knowledge.

Identifying Design Models and Project Mapping Strategies

Most design models share some common components but will also have specific actionable steps that adapt to the idea. As an example, Design Thinking is a methodology used to solve complex problems and find desirable solutions. This model is beneficial because it begins with empathy where observation and engaging with those affected by a problem or idea becomes the centerpiece for identifying and defining the project. Design Thinking utilizes several steps that draws upon logic, intuition, creative thinking, imagination and reasoning to explore possibilities of what could be and create desired outcomes.

Other design models such as the Engineering Design Model or If-Then Planning Model provide succinct processes for moving ideas along and getting things done. Both models are proven to be effective and can be used by individuals or groups.

The Engineering Design Model

The Engineer Design Model follows a flow of six steps that takes an idea from conception to completion. The model can be adaptive as a process in instructional activities for children or modified to accommodate special projects. Logical progressive steps:

1. *Define the problem*
2. *Gather information*
3. *Brainstorm and analyze ideas*
4. *Develop solutions*
5. *Gather feedback*
6. *Improve (as needed)*

It is easy to see how these steps can move an idea along and provide outputs that can be evaluated to determine if a product or developed idea is reliable.

The If-Then Model

The If-Then Model is a simple strategy that can be used to achieve any goal by deciding in advance when and where to take specific actions that support goal attainment. It outlines constructs based on thoughts that incorporate "if"/ "then" or "when/then" to redirect habits or events that may be distracting from productivity. (If its 5:00, then I will meet review and return calls). It's pre-planning for "cause and effect" possibilities, which may apply to personal or organizational distractions. As example, (If colleagues meet in the lounge for coffee at 9:00 - then I will get coffee at 8:00; When I get to work at 8:00, then I will get coffee from the lounge). Using this approach is not intended to serve to avoid social contact with colleagues for controlling individual time on task. This can be a great benefit for a thought leadership cohort as a tool maintaining focus and time on tasks during group sessions.

Process Mapping

Process mapping is one of many tools that can be used to streamline the work and associated tasks into a smooth and efficient manner. It covers the entire scope of the project, checks alignment with goals and desired standards, measures progress and pays close attention to expected time frames for completing tasks. Process mapping is most effective when organized as a visual illustration, so it will be necessary to create a design, but one that is flexible to allow adaptations as needed. Cohort members will need to receive training on appropriate designs, but utilizing design that incorporate concept mapping, mind mapping, outlining and visual mapping will aid in getting ideas from an abstract to concrete state. Microsoft templates or platforms such as Smartsheets are excellent tools to start the process for hashing out new ideas and planning any change strategy or project.

Strategy 9: Employ Kurt Lewin's Change Theory to clarify what changes are needed, implement change and sustain change.

"If you truly want to understand something, try to change it."

Kurt Lewin

If you have a large cube of ice, but realize that you want several ice cubes, what do you do? You can use a large blunt object to strike and shatter the ice into pieces. Another choice would be to allow time for the ice to melt, making it amenable to change (unfreeze). Then you need to mold the iced water into new shapes by pouring it in trays (change). Finally, you must solidify the new shape (refreeze). According to Kurt Lewin Model, this process can be adapted to any situation where change is a target goal. Lewin, developed the Change Theory in 1940's, but today it remains as a compelling strategy for managing change. Lewin Change Theory consist of three stages:

- *Unfreeze: Identify the behavior, skill or habit that would benefit from change.*
- *Change: replace the behavior, skill or habit by doing something different.*
- *Refreeze: Solidify the new behavior, skill or habit by practicing and utilizing it often.*

The three stages would appear simple and easy to accomplish, but it is extremely difficult to achieve each stage because of what Lewin refers to as Force Field Analysis. Lewin surmised that change is slow due to conflicting forces that influence decisions that support or detract from the intended goal. His model shows that individuals or factors contribute to a dynamic that affect equilibrium in change initiatives.

Figure 2.1

Kurt Lewin - Force Field Analysis

Restraining Forces	Proposed Change	Driving Forces
These forces are pulling away from the intended change.		These forces are supporting change.

Employing Lewin's Change Theory is a fundamental aspect of thought leadership since the primary intent is to change mindsets. Influencing and managing change requires that individuals participate in selective change in processes that may be embedded in daily activities. Difficulties may result from internal or external factors that lead to work as well as emotional stressors, requiring change management. A recent survey of CEO's reports that up to 75% of their organizational change efforts fail to yield the promised results. Consequently, influencing change could be a primary role for cohorts since change management encompasses disrupting the status quo, moving ideas along, consensus building, getting buy in and codifying systems that sustain new discoveries. Thought leadership recognizes that all components in change are critically important because organizations don't change, people do. Change management also represents the essence of what thought leaders accomplish. As author C.D. Jackson notes, "Great ideas need landing gear as well as wings". Thought leadership provides both.

Questions for Reflection: Ask yourself...

1. *Why does our organization need change?*

2. *What benefits and value will change impact for the organization?*

3. *How will individual members benefit from change?*

4. *What happens if we wait before approaching change?*

5. *What resources are needed to initiate change?*

6. *Who will we need to initiate change?*

Epilogue

Get in Where You Fit In

"Start by doing what is necessary; then do the possible; and suddenly you are doing the impossible."- Francis of Assisi

I am uncertain about who coined the phrase, "get in where you fit in", or why but in my perspective, it is an ideal way to conclude a discussion about thought leadership as a strategy for organizations. This section provides an overview for leaders interested in aligning this fascinating concept to move along ideas.

This effort was intended to provide a snapshot view of how thought leadership can ignite, activate and facilitate in any organization. In keeping with this goal, we conclude with a few benefits of thought leadership that will hopefully activate interest of readers in pursuing this fascinating phenomenon in great details. So, individuals, start- up business, educational institutions, social entrepreneurs, public entities, corporations or organized groups, get in where you fit in with the idea of thought leadership, but don't stop there, keep asking "what if" and "why not" questions. Discover "who's in" that is willing to support your goals and Let's Go!

A Few Benefits of Employing Thought Leadership Cohorts As A Strategy For Schools

"Learning is an engagement of the mind that changes the mind."

Martin Heidegger

1. *Improves critical thinking - Thought leadership can train brains to think faster and sharper.*

2. *Enhances thought management and compliant behavior - Thought*

leadership can help students learn the skill of managing thoughts to reduce spontaneous inappropriate non-compliant actions.

3. *Improves student motivation - A student's input can galvanize an otherwise skeptical teacher to make changes.*

4. *Engages student participation - Students have unique perspectives and insight to contribute to changes that will impact their daily activities.*

5. *Improves buy-in - Students have an arsenal of tools that can be used to sabotage the best-intentioned reform efforts when they have no buy-in.*

6. *Improves opportunities for active inquiry and experiential Learning -Students should play an active role in determining pathways to learning.*

7. *Fosters a sense of belonging in school as a community Youth involvement is consistent with democratic ideals of shared representation and participation of all stakeholders.*

8. *Enhances opportunities for participative leadership and collective thought - One central organizing principle of leadership is that, "success cannot be achieved alone." Whether the organization includes five people or 50,000 people, the complexities of human motivation will defy any attempt to take a one-size-fits-all approach to leadership or efforts to achieve goals.*

9. *Enhances leadership skills - Student involvement in school reform enhances leadership development and ownership of what is occurring during change.*

10. *Improves buy in to change ideas - The challenges involved in modifying and codifying an organization's culture are immense. Organizational*

members and many stakeholders are typically inherently resistant to radical change.

11. *Enhance opportunities for inclusion in student reform initiatives - Student input in school reform is frequently limited to evaluations about the quality of teachers. Failure to incorporate students' perceptions when redesigning change in a learning environment leads to feelings of alienation and disempowerment among students, with consequential adverse effects on motivation.*

12. *Enhances learning - Education should operate as a process of continuous group discussion (dialogue) that enables people to acquire collective knowledge that they can use to grow, influence and impact.*

Finally, thought Leadership as a strategy to promote change in schools will likely become contagious because the best change agents are often great minds, sitting next to each other who share ideas, and are willing to assist each other?

For Organizations

The use of thought leadership cohorts can be an asset for any type of business or organization but is especially beneficial to improve efforts of start-up or small companies with limited financial resources by building human capacity as an asset.

1. *The use of thought leadership cohort is a great way to move ideas along.*

2. *Cohorts serve as a structured platform to influence followers to support the organization's vision and goals.*

3. *Cohorts enhance opportunities for building and sustaining "learning organizations".*

4. *Cohorts can provide strategies that create sustainable outcomes.*

5. *Cohorts offer opportunities for participative leadership.*

6. *Cohorts enhance opportunities for building/sustaining "learning organizations".*

7. *The use of cohorts embraces diversity and inclusive work spaces.*

8. *Cohorts provides a voice for subgroups and stakeholders*

9. *Leaders utilizing cohorts demonstrate that employee have value*

10. *Improves human capacity for the organization.*

11. *Enhances opportunities for creativity around ideas.*

12. *Promotes an awareness and acceptance of system-thinking.*

13. *Cohorts can support change initiatives and encourage buy-in.*

In summary, leadership is about creating compelling ideas that promote growth, inclusion, productivity, excellence and a profitable bottom line. Employing principles of thought leaders can advance the flow of ideas and ultimately set an organization apart one that is unique and maintain a competitive edge in influencing mindsets.

References

Blustein, B. L., (2006). The psychology of working: A new perspective for career development, counseling and public policy. London, New Jersey: Mahwah, Lawrence Erlbaum Associates Publishers.

Clark, D., "How to Become a Top Business Thinker", Forbes, July 21, 2014.www.forbes.com/sites/dorieclark/2014/07/21/ho-to-be-a-top-business-thinker/.

Clark, D., (2015) Stand Out – How to Find Your Breakthrough Idea and Build a Following Around It. Penguin Publishing Group. New York, NY.

Follett, M.P. (1949/1987). 'The Essentials of Leadership', in L. Urwick(ed.) Freedom and Co-ordination: Lectures in Business Organization, New York: Garland Publishing.

Johnson, MD, Spencer, (1998). Who Moved My Cheese, G.P. Putman's Sons, New York, NY

Maxwell, J. C., (2009). How Successful People Think, Center Street Publishing, New York, NY.

Rath, T. (2007). Strength Finders-2.0. Gallup Press, New York, N.Y.

Schein, E.H., (2010). Organizational culture and Leadership

Senge, P. (2006). The Fifth Discipline- The Art & Practice of the Learning Organization, Doubleday, New York, N. Y.

Stogill, R. M., (1974). Handbook of Leadership: A Survey of Literature, New York Free Press

Wakefield, M., Bunker, KA. (2009). The center for creative leadership: Handbook for leadership development. Chapter 7. Greensboro, North Carolina: Josey-Bass

Velsor, E., McCauley, C.D., Ruderman, M.N. (2010). Handbook for Leadership Development: The Center for Creative Leadership, John Wiley & Sons, San Francisco, CA. Yukl, G., (2006). Leadership in organizations. Upper Saddle River, NJ: Pearson-Prentice Hall.